Edisol Dotson

Behold the Man
The Hype and Selling of Male Beauty in Media and Culture

Pre-publication
REVIEW

"A nd we thought only women were enslaved by the beauty myth! In this captivating work—part historical and sociological analysis, part stinging indictment—Dotson makes clear how American men have also been drawn into the culture of self-hatred that fuels the myth."

Michael Kimmel, PhD
Professor of Sociology,
State University of New York
at Stony Brook;
Author, *Manhood in America*

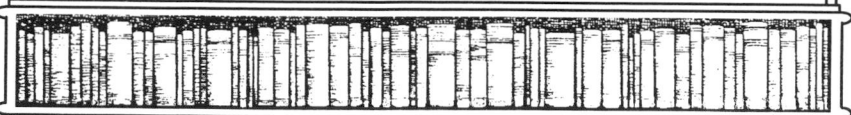

Behold the Man
The Hype and Selling of Male Beauty in Media and Culture

HAWORTH Gay & Lesbian Studies
John P. De Cecco, PhD
Editor in Chief

Behold the Man

The Hype and Selling of Male Beauty in Media and Culture

Edisol Wayne Dotson

Harrington Park Press
An Imprint of The Haworth Press, Inc.
New York • London

Published by

Harrington Park Press, an imprint of The Haworth Press, Inc., 10 Alice Street, Binghamton, NY 13904-1580

The Haworth Press, Inc., 10 Alice Street, Binghamton, NY 13904-1580

Cover design by Marylouise E. Doyle.

The Library of Congress has cataloged the hardcover edition of this book as:

Dotson, Edisol W.
  Behold the man : the hype and selling of male beauty in media and culture / Edisol Wayne Dotson.
      p.   cm.
  Includes bibliographical references and index.
  ISBN 0-7890-0634-0 (alk. paper)
  1. Masculinity. 2. Beauty, Personal. 3. Masculinity in popular culture. 4. Men in mass media. 5. Men in literature. 6. Male nude in art. I. Title.
HQ1090.D675 1999
305.31—dc21   98-39345
                                                                                                      CIP

ISBN 1-56023-953-0 (pbk.)

To Alisa Weiner, Will Federico, and Tom Squire

ABOUT THE AUTHOR

Edisol Wayne Dotson is a writer living in San Francisco, California, whose fiction has appeared in *Christopher Street, New York Native,* and *Art & Understanding.* Dotson's nonfiction has been published in the *San Francisco Sentinel* and the *Bay Area Reporter.* In addition, he is the editor of *Putting Out: The Essential Publishing Resource for Lesbian and Gay Writers.*

CONTENTS

Preface

There are two reasons why I wrote this book. First, there is my body and what it means to me and to others. Second, there is a fear inside me that the male body is being used as a gauge against which men's worth and role in society are being measured.

It has only been in the last five years or so that I have managed to find a level of comfort with who and what I am physically. Before this, there seemed always to be something wrong with the way I looked. There was a time when I thought my hair, for example, was too curly and kinky. When not cut, it grew into an Afro. An Afro may have been acceptable for a white man in the 1970s; it was also enough to earn me the dubious title of "Bozo the Clown." Only when I began to mature and subsequently learned the meaning of "vanity" was I able to shed this title. I discovered the "beauty salon" and what it could do for my hair. Little did I know that having my hair styled, instead of letting it be what it was naturally, was only the beginning of my trip through vanity.

It was, after all, my face and what it looked like that seemed to matter and be important when looking for sexual and emotional partners. I naturally assumed that the face I looked at when seeking these companions for myself was the same for those looking at me. I started experimenting with having my eyelashes tinted, whitening my teeth, and giving the illusion that I had high cheekbones by using bronzer. I even experimented with cosmetics, subtle shades of eyeliner and eye shadow. Why did I do all of this? I was hooked on looking at the men in *Gentlemen's Quarterly* and decided that I had to look like them. Only then could I consider myself handsome or attractive, and worthy of someone's attention.

It wasn't until I moved to San Francisco in 1986 that I realized there was much more at issue than my face. The turning point came one day when I was walking through the Castro and passed by a shop selling coffee beans and cheeses. Taped in the window were pages torn from magazines. They were photographs of men nearly naked, with rippling stomachs and smooth, firm pectorals. They had the *GQ* faces, but they had much more—something I clearly did not have.

It was not the photographs themselves or even the men that caught my eye and made me stop. I was accustomed to seeing photographs of naked, well-built men in the magazines and newspapers I read. I accepted them as a matter of course. I merely thought that was the way my media was managed, and because I was so "into" being gay, I didn't question it.

What turned me down a new road (and perhaps even turned my stomach a bit) was that these photographs were hanging in the window of a shop selling coffee beans and cheeses—*coffee beans and cheeses*. This marrying of near-naked male bodies with these particular products struck me as absurd. What possible connection could there be?

The shop owner's tactics worked, at least in part. Although I did not go inside to make a purchase, I had stopped and gazed. Since I liked what I saw, might I, the next time I needed coffee beans or cheese, remember these men and be drawn back to this particular shop? Is this the power of suggestion in advertising?

That single incident had such an enormous effect on me that I became more aware of nudity in gay male culture. It didn't take long to notice that it—nudity—was everywhere I looked. I could not escape it. I realized that the men in those photographs hanging in the window of the coffee beans/cheese shop looked almost identical in body type to the men I saw in advertisements, pornography, greeting cards, calendars, newspapers, magazines, films, and at the gym. More important, I became aware that my body did not look like the ones that were so obviously being espoused as the ideal body type.

Up until then, my body was simply that—my body. I was, after all, sexually active and drew no correlation between what my body looked like and my ability or desire to have sex. I had no reason to believe I was being denied my fair share of sexual activity.

Then the realization hit home: If I had a body like the ones I kept seeing in the various arenas of my culture, could I have even *more* sex? Even better, could I then find and keep someone to love me and therefore make me complete and happy?

My thin body, wholly lacking in muscular development, suddenly became a source of embarrassment. It was obvious that I was not the gay male ideal. It occurred to me that I had rejected potential partners, both sexual and emotional, based solely on what they looked like and that perhaps I had been rejected for the very same reason.

This was when I first began to be afraid. If I could be made to feel that I am in some way physically inferior or undesirable, were other men being made to feel the same way?

I am afraid that too many men, straight and gay, do not realize how perspectives have changed with respect to the roles and portrayals of the male body in the elements of our culture and society. I am afraid of how quiet we are when it comes to discussing how the male body is projected as an object of sex. Too many continue to believe this to be a problem only women need to worry about.

By disassociating from gay male culture and from culture in general, I discovered that the notion of being a man is dependent more and more upon certain predetermined or predefined definitions and characteristics. I had to step away from the worlds in which I was so deeply entrenched. I had to stop going to the gym before I realized that what I was trying to accomplish by lifting weights was to make my body more desirable to other men.

After reading Naomi Wolf's *The Beauty Myth*, I began to notice the men around me. As a gay man, it seemed natural to do so. However, instead of looking at them as potential mates, I saw them as something more—men who, like me, were in danger of being judged solely on the look of their faces and bodies.

Wolf's book also made me aware of how women are treated in media and culture and, subsequently, in real life. Admittedly, I was shocked at what she had to say. I was also embarrassed, realizing that I, too, had played a part in the subordination of women. Being a gay man does not make me blind to female beauty and desirability.

I started to pay more attention to the way women were portrayed in films, television programs, and especially, advertising. I found myself looking beyond the clothing and accessories, the perfumes, and the jewelry. What I discovered was the women and their bodies. I was horrified and began to wonder what younger women and little girls were seeing when they viewed those same images. I considered myself more fortunate than they because I did not have to grow up and try to become what society dictates.

By examining magazines and publications aimed at straight men and, in particular, by watching television commercials broadcast during football games and other sporting events, I began to see men in the straight world portrayed as they are in the gay world. The gay fantasy/ideal became the straight fantasy/ideal. There he was on my TV screen, shaving or washing his hair or drinking beer on the beach, and generally, his chest was exposed, forcing me to look at my own in comparison.

I am afraid other men, too many men, are doing the same thing—looking at themselves in comparison. I am afraid they are wondering whether they measure up to the men they see on their TV screens, or in their magazines, or as they sit in a movie theater and watch yet another male actor expose his body. I am afraid, too, that women view these same images and are either snickering in smugness or suddenly questioning the attractiveness and worth of their husbands or partners.

Most of all, I am afraid for the younger men and boys growing up in a world in which muscles equal manliness. What must they think as they flip through their comic books and see their heroes, with bodies often exaggerated in their muscularity? What must they think when they see these same heroes on movie screens—the actors' bodies stuffed into sculpted rubber suits or pumped up enough to fill out body-hugging costumes? I feel sorry for these boys, particularly when I see television commercials for acne medications telling teenage boys who have acne that they are not welcome, not wanted. They can forget about going to the spring dance or to the prom. No girl wants to be seen with them.

In writing this book, I am attempting to expose a problem that I believe exists in our society: too many men are listening to the silent images of faces and bodies represented in media and culture and are consequently receiving a very strict set of guidelines that must be met to be acceptable—to be considered men.

Edisol Wayne Dotson

Acknowledgments

I would like to thank the people who contributed to the process of writing this book. Sincere thanks to Michael Tomczak, Steve White, Philip Leider, Richard Labonté, and Michael O'Brien for reading the early drafts and for giving me new and different perspectives from which to write. Thanks also to Will Federico, Lynn Borowitz, Alison Scott, Tom Squire, Anthony Turney, Alisa Weiner, Kirk Kleinschmidt, Lasse van Essen, Howard Walseman, Philip Polivchak, Kimberly Allen, Al Kamikawa, Jeff Monford, Ben Thompson, Nancy Fax, Matthew Kennedy, and Maurice Kelly for listening to me ramble on about what writing this book means to me.

I am grateful to the staff at The Haworth Press, particularly Bill Palmer, John De Cecco, Peg Marr, and Amy Rentner, for their help in preparing the manuscript for publication.

I am grateful also for the knowledge and contributions of others who have written on this subject, particularly Naomi Wolf, Susan Faludi, Susan Jeffords, Michael Nava, Brian Pronger, Samuel Wilson Fussell, Anthony Easthope, Allan M. Klein, Kenneth Clark, Margaret Walters, Melody D. Davis, Michael Kimmel, and Frank Browning. It was, after all, listening to what others have to say that made it possible for me to hear and better understand what I have to say.

Finally, I wish to thank Pam Ahearn for her belief in the book and for her efforts on its behalf.

Introduction

Masculinity, or manliness—whatever we choose to call it—is a cultural creation. Every culture, and every subculture, probably has its own idealized image of masculinity or manliness. Such ideas, although culturally created, need not be culturally bound; they can easily be lifted from one culture and placed in another.

Because of this borrowing between cultures, writing this book without including data and information on gay *and* straight males would have made the book incomplete, biased, and unfair. To concentrate solely on one culture of men and not another would be seen as an attack on a particular group of men. The purpose of this book is not to attack anyone. Rather, it is an investigation of those who are responsible, in part or in whole, for creating and defining culturally accepted ideals of male beauty and how we, the general public, accept them with little resistance.

Likewise, to write this book without looking at cultural representations of women would have made the book lopsided. Male beauty would never have become an issue if it were not for the attention given to female beauty. A men's movement would not have been born without a preceding women's movement. Issues of masculinity would never have been scrutinized if issues of femininity had not been placed so much in the world's view. The danger here is that this reversal of attention will further divide the sexes and do nothing to bring them together.

Too many women are enjoying what is happening to men. Too many men are confused about issues of physical beauty as an idealized trait of masculinity. Words such as beautiful, masculine, handsome, and attractive are becoming far too commonplace when describing males. These terms have become less a way of describing men and more a way of defining them as ideal husbands, fathers, lovers, or simply as being worthy. Where does this leave the ordinary man who cannot see himself as those extraordinary men selling beer and shaving products? Where does this leave the man who cannot imagine himself pictured on the cover of *Gentlemen's Quarterly*?

This book is also about the business of male beauty, offering details and evidence that it is a booming business. Recent reports indicate that American men spend *$9.5 billion* annually to improve their appearance. Surely, with this phenomenal amount of money being spent, male beauty is not an issue that can be easily ignored.

Beyond the beauty industry, there are other industries and additional areas of our culture in which men, alongside women, are being stereotyped, objectified, and exploited. This book investigates the worlds of art, fiction, advertising, films, television, music, pornography, cosmetic surgery, eating disorders, and bodybuilding. The chapters set out to identify those areas of our culture in which certain types of male bodies are objectified to become nothing more than images of ideal partners.

The male body has become the subject of intense cultural and societal scrutiny. As with the female body, the meaning of the male body has been redefined as more than an identifier of sex or gender. The male body alone, in all its shapes and sizes, fails to establish that men are men purely by virtue of their maleness. This book takes the dominating characteristics of modern-day society and brings them together. By looking at these elements, one after the other, it becomes obvious that the stereotyping of the male body is not an isolated occurrence. If it were, there would be no reason for this book to exist, and male body idealization could be dismissed as merely a trend. However, male body stereotyping is too cross-cultural, too common, too *expected* to be considered a trend. It is not a matter of *one* underwear or cologne ad, *one* book, or *one* film. It is a matter of a continuing succession of these elements that have become so entrenched in our society, that they seem to be here to stay.

Chapter 1

Where We Are

Men are meat—their naked bodies hoisted up on larger-than-life billboards, flashed across movie and television screens, frozen in print advertisements, displayed as props and playthings in music videos, begged for in pornography, silenced in erotica, shamed into dieting, chopped up in cosmetic surgery centers. Words such as objectification, glorification, exploitation, and stereotyping come to mind. These words once rang as battle cries from women who were sick and tired of having their bodies turned into plastic toys. These words that helped spark a movement toward equality are words of war.

No battle or movement is fought or won without casualties. Men are beginning to lose what women have begun to gain in the war against the depiction and treatment of human bodies. The difference, however, is that most men probably do not realize what their bodies are being put through. Women are not offered the same luxury because the power structure continues to favor men. It is mostly the male power structure that makes demands and places expectations on the appearance of the female body. Women react with extreme body-altering activities—excessive exercise or dieting or cosmetic surgery—so they and their bodies can meet the demands and live up to the expectations issued by men.

Yet, as the decades continue to unfold, the power structure is beginning to crack just enough to allow women the opportunity to enter its domain. Although the power women have gained is minute in scope and scale when compared to the amount of power still held by men, women's power is nonetheless present. Power, even in small amounts, brings privilege in our society. Some women now find themselves in a position in which *they* can make demands and place expectations on the appearance of the bodies of the opposite sex.

How one views the body and appearance of the opposite sex is a component of the power structure, and more and more men are finding themselves suddenly on the other side of the viewing stand. This of course does not mean that a balance in power has been established. Men are still in control when it comes to high-power or high-profile careers, higher incomes, and wide-reaching or unilateral decision making. A challenge to men's hold on this power exists but continues to be seen more as a nuisance than an actual threat. Men see the *possibility* of losing this power but are not overly concerned with the loss becoming a reality—not yet, anyway.

Even though the bodies of women continue to be splayed across the canvases of media and popular culture as the ideal of feminine perfection, alongside them are the bodies of men, equally naked, equally perfect.

Maleness, now less identified and symbolized by historically or biologically assigned characteristics—fulfilling the role of bread-winner or the possession of a penis—has become a multifaceted and multidefined existence that includes ever-changing and often confusing ideas of masculinity. More important, altered ideologies of male physical appearance and male beauty play a pivotal role in the search for masculine identification.

More and more we are seeing naked or near-naked male bodies in print advertisements and television commercials, using the male body solely as a means to grab the consumer's attention. Male bodies shown in these advertisements are obviously chosen for their appearance of facial beauty and muscularity. An ideal is created, mass-produced, and then disseminated throughout the population.

Today, partly as a result of the women's movement and partly due to the changing roles of men in society, images of beautiful men have firmly established the standards of what men must look like to meet the criteria of being desirable. In short, the male image has been reduced to a four-letter word—hunk. If men are not hunks—or clever enough to hide their unmanly or unmuscular bodies with the right clothing—they are led to believe that they stand little or no chance of achieving or emulating the emotional and sexual satisfaction illustrated in the cultural images surrounding them.

A concern for male beauty, once regarded as a trait of questionable sexuality, has been introduced fully into heterosexual culture. As they did so successfully with women, the male beauty molders of Madison Avenue and Hollywood are forcing images of men onto the general population which are causing men to alter their self-perceptions and which are in turn causing women to change their perceptions of men. These images have created a dramatic shift in what it takes for men to compete in changing cultural, social, sexual, and professional societies.

THE NEW MAN EMERGES

Beauty is a business, a huge money-making industry, feeding and surviving on the low self-esteem of women and men. The beauty industry, an expansive amalgamation of several image-oriented industries, creates low self-esteem by distorting reality to the degree that both women and men find it increasingly difficult to distinguish between truth and fantasy. Million-dollar profits are earned by the beauty industry by exploiting the vulnerabilities and insecurities of women and men, telling them they are not beautiful enough to survive in today's world. But, if you buy our products or pay for the services we offer, the beauty industry says, we will make you beautiful, we will make you worthy, we will make you successful, we will make you sexy. Women's magazines have been doing this for years. They have set what Naomi Wolf calls in *The Beauty Myth* "the beauty index."[1] Cosmetic and plastic surgeons have done the same. So too have advertisers, movie, television, and music video producers, and writers and other artists. Having firmly established themselves as leaders of a beauty cult, mainly at the expense of women, industries and professionals have turned their attention to men. It isn't that these industries have stopped creating and re-creating beautiful women; they have now set their eyes on creating the perfect complement to beautiful women: beautiful men.

Recent reports indicate that men are spending $3.3 billion annually on grooming products such as fragrances, deodorants, and hair-coloring treatments. Another $4.27 billion is spent on gym/health club memberships, exercise equipment, and exercise machines for the stomach muscles. Bald men or men losing their hair now spend $1.36 billion annually, mainly on transplants, wigs, and hair-restoration treatments. An additional $507 million is spent on cosmetic surgery procedures.[2] These staggering amounts of money clearly indicate that the desire to be beautiful in our society is no longer a desire particular to women only.

Only within the last decade or so has notice of the male body, beyond its clothes, hair, and face, been pushed to the forefront of cultural observation. Now, how men look without their clothes is essential to who they are, what they become, where they go, whom they marry, and with whom they have sex.

In 1989, *Psychology Today* printed an article summarizing data from a survey they had previously published on identifying the current version of an idealized male body. The article concluded that neither men nor women expressed concern for the size of a man's chest, only for a man's desire to remain committed to the family unit and to his own growth.[3] In 1993, the same magazine offered another survey asking for its readers' opinions on the male physique. At the beginning of the survey, the authors state that a sudden concern for the physical appearance of male bodies came about because of shifting roles of men and women in society.[4] In four short years, a well-respected publication, aimed at an intelligent, sophisticated readership, went from finding men and women not being concerned about male physical appearance to asking their male readership questions about the importance of muscles on the male body and their female readership questions about the relationship between being attracted to a man and the presence of muscles on a man's body?[5] Why did this shift in curiosity in what constitutes the ideal male occur? What happened between 1989 and 1993 to make a publication such as *Psychology Today* become concerned about whether men and women pay attention to muscles on the male body?

In 1987, *Cosmopolitan* magazine printed an article titled "What Makes a Man Sexy Today?" The author opens her discussion by relating a story of meeting a man on a plane whom she describes as looking "like a kid" and "scrawny." Because of these visual qualifications, she assumes the man is gay. When at dinner the man admits to her that he is flirting, the author writes, "I changed my perception of his body from scrawny to compact." The scrawny kid who she thought was gay was suddenly someone with whom she wanted to have sex. She wanted to have sex with him not because she found him physically attractive or even manly, but because his flirting had reached her on a level beyond mere physical attraction.[6]

Further into the article, the author establishes criteria for assessing a man's sexiness. She lists intelligence, confidence, trust, wealth (and, in some cases, even poverty), all as being attributes which a man can possess that will make him sexy in ways mere good looks cannot.[7] In 1987, according to *Cosmopolitan*, women were not overly concerned with the look of the male body.

Two years later, in an article published in *Muscle & Fitness* titled "What Makes a Man Sexy? Muscles, Mostly," the author counters the *Cosmopolitan* article by saying that what women want, without question, are men who have muscular bodies. There is little in this article about spiritual connections between men and women; nothing about scrawny kids suspected of being gay who become suddenly sexy enough to hump on the dinner table.[8]

Why this disparity in opinions on what makes a man sexy? What compels these two writers to be at such opposite ends of the spectrum when it comes to sexy men? The first writer nearly goes out of her way to avoid making good looks and muscles attributes of male sexiness, while the latter waxes at length on the delights, even the necessity, of those same good looks and muscles.

* * *

This is where we are—men in the forefront of cultural scrutiny. Men's bodies are carefully examined from head to toe. What's at stake? Men's self-esteem, self-worth, and their acceptance or rejection as suitable partners.

Chapter 2

Fine Lines:
Painting, Sculpture, and Photography

To give a history of the male body as represented in art is beyond the scope of this book. The sampling provided here does illustrate, however, that the male nude in art cannot be ignored or rejected as having had some influence on how we view the male body. Male bodies depicted in historical sculptures and paintings in the societies in which they were created, and subsequently in other societies, hold the same meanings as present-day images of male bodies in our culture's visual media.

There is little difference in idealized male beauty in art of the past and art of today. Male bodies then, as they are now, were superior only if they were muscular and well-proportioned. Historical heroes, immortalized in stone, marble, bronze, and paint, were men of strength, the muscles of their bodies rippling in battle or exultation. We can be certain there were no statues of obese men standing in the great halls and monuments of ancient Greece and Rome.

It is difficult to imagine a time when the naked human body was not objectified in works of art, either intentionally by modern day artists or unintentionally by those who painted stick figures on cave walls. For centuries, both male and female naked bodies have been viewed as symbols of good and evil, divine and material, right and wrong, moral and immoral. From the beginning of time, the naked body has lain at or very near the center of humankind's quest for the meaning of life. For centuries, historians, scholars, philosophers, scientists, artists, writers, poets, and laymen have tried to determine what role the human body plays in our day-to-day lives and what it means to us when we view the body naked. Is the human body a source of pleasure and beauty, or is it a source of sin and shame? In history, it has been both. It is in art that we find the best and most accurate clues to how the naked human body has been perceived and received throughout the ages.

THE EARLY AESTHETES

There is no evidence to suggest that prehistoric men or women had any reverence or admiration for the male body, not at least in the way we, as modern humans, revere and admire male flesh.

The Greek ideal of male beauty, on the other hand, has influenced artists and nonartists alike for thousands of years. Since the time of the ancient Greeks, most of the notable artists interested in the male nude as subject matter have drawn on classic Greek ideals of the male form and have incorporated these ideals into their own artistic representations.

The nonartists, those who view art rather than create it, also use the comparison of classical Greek art in their everyday references to male beauty. Often we hear someone saying, when describing a man, "He is like a Greek god" or "His body looks like a Greek statue," or, simply, "He is a god." According to art historian Kenneth Clark, author of *The Nude: A Study in Ideal Form*, "the perfect human body" in Greek art appeared around 480 B.C. Twenty-five-hundred years later, this body is still with us, still displaying and describing for us the man of our dreams.[1]

Although the youthful male was by far the archetype of male beauty in Greek culture, Greek artists, through their art, sought to perfect even the most common man by making the claim that the forms depicted in their art embodied the look of all Greek citizens.[2] Not much has changed in 2,500 years.

Although ancient Greek cultures exist only in scattered ruins, in history books, and in the world of make-believe created by the film and television industries, the embodiment of the perfected male form found throughout the history of Greek art is as real today as it was 2,500 years ago. We continue to create the male form in art and base its appearance on either what we think or what we are told is the ideal male form.

THE RENAISSANCE OF MAN

Perhaps more than any of the rest, the work of Michelangelo has had the most lasting effect on us as we search for historical definitions of ideal male beauty and a perfect male body. Art historians have much to say about Michelangelo and his artistic renderings of the male body and seem to give him as much credit for heralding and defining the superiority of the male body as all of the Greek artists combined.[3]

To have his body compared to Michelangelo's *David*, or almost any of Michelangelo's nude figures, is one of the greatest compliments a modern man can receive. As a work of art, Michelangelo's *David* may or may not be perfect. As an ideal of male beauty, however, it is. Michelangelo did for his time what the Greeks did for theirs: he perfected man in art as a reflection of how a real man should look, or should wish to look, in life.

Alongside Michelangelo was Leonardo da Vinci, certainly no stranger to creating the ideal male form in art. His most famous drawing of the male figure is his *Vitruvian Man*, the naked male figure encased in a circle and square. Here, in an attempt to create and justify the perfect male body, Leonardo reduced physical appearance to mathematics, a method handed down from the Greeks.

Being a scientist and an artist, Leonardo was as interested in how the male body worked as in how it looked. To better understand the workings of the male body, he, along with his contemporaries, took up human dissection. It is said that Michelangelo attempted dissection in his quest to fully know the workings of the male body but could not stomach the process.[4]

Leonardo continued with his dissections and, from what he saw, produced drawings called "a tribute to the complex beauty of the body" that turned "the body into a marvelous machine." The male body of today is often compared to or presented as a machine. But unlike the machines of Leonardo, the modern-day machine is so called because of its outward appearance—its muscularity.[5]

We can only imagine what Michelangelo and Leonardo might have thought of modern-day cosmetic surgery. These artists, in many ways, were precursors of twentieth-century plastic and cosmetic surgeons. In their time, Michelangelo and Leonardo could not cut up and then rearrange the male body in flesh as surgeons do today; they could, however, have the next best thing, by cutting up the body and reconfiguring it in their paintings and sculptures. Were they alive today, we might find them holding a scalpel instead of a chisel or paintbrush.

MODERN HEROES

The twentieth century is not without its own artistic concept of idealized male appearance. To truly understand how the perfected ideal of male physical beauty has been revived in this century to influence the way we perceive beauty, one only has to examine the propagandist art of Nazi Germany, the "lowest point . . . in the obscene, plastic perfection of publicity and propaganda."[6] Adolph Hitler and those who worked under him were the masters of propaganda art. Their espousal of human (Aryan) glorification and purity through extreme physical strength and muscularity was a major political/propaganda component of Nazi Germany.

Artists who lived during the years of Nazi reign were forbidden to depict the male body as anything but a superior being. Artists who broke this rule were considered degenerates, their right to paint or sculpt was revoked, and their work was confiscated and often destroyed. Hitler would allow no work of art that did not promote his concept of idealized beauty and masculinity.

Josef Thorak's *Monument to the Freedom of Danzig* (1943), a sculpted man of Herculean proportions, clearly shows that the Nazi ideal of male perfection is no different from the ancient Greek ideal, nor from the one in late-twentieth-century society. Susan Bordo makes this very clear in her essay, "Reading the Male Body," in which she writes that today's idealized male bodies ". . . are starting to look more and more like those depicted in Nazi posters and sculptures."[7]

Were Hitler alive today, he would make a powerful and successful advertising executive. His tactics of using artistic representations to shape our concepts of the ideal male form are still with us, not as political propaganda, but as social propaganda.

ART AS SEX

Because we are bombarded with sexual imagery in so many aspects of our modern lives, it is often difficult for us to look at a naked body in art without attaching a sexual meaning to it. We find ourselves aroused rather than appreciating the representation as a work of art. Women and gay men view the naked man as a sexual interest or disinterest, accepting or dismissing him, based upon supposed personal taste. Women and gay men may find themselves comparing their real life sexual partners to those they see in works of art. Straight men, although not sexually interested in what they see, are forced to look at their own bodies and wonder if they are living up to the physical expectations of their female partners and of society in general.

Gay men find themselves having to compare not only their real life sexual partners but also themselves. Art serves as both mirror and instruction manual. Art aimed at a gay male audience poses great danger for gay men because the men depicted in this very specialized market are often created with overly exaggerated muscles and genitals.

The work of Tom of Finland is the most obvious example of this. Perhaps more than any other artistic works (with the possible exception of some of Robert Mapplethorpe's photographs), Tom of Finland tests the limit of what separates art from pornography—and certainly would send arts-funding establishments such as the National Endowment for the Arts into a wild tailspin. The focal point of a great many of his works is the penis, either gargantuan in its naked display or teasingly tucked away, but no less noticeable or large, in tight trousers or shorts. Peniscs of the size illustrated in thc drawings of Tom of Finland are grossly inflated and somewhat unrealistic. Undoubtedly, there are *some* men *somewhere* who have extra large penises, but their numbers are few when compared to the number of men who are average, or even above average, in size. To depict overly muscular men with oversized penises as the typical gay male fantasy is the projection of a stereotype. Paintings, drawings, or photographs of women with extremely large breasts are not accurate depictions of women's bodies and are not tolerated. Similarly, men should not have to tolerate false depictions of muscles and penises.

Tom of Finland is not the only artist who uses art to showcase an idealized or fantasized male body and its parts. Texas artist Delmas Howe is another. What makes Howe's work most interesting is not so much the type of bodies his nudes project, although they are muscled and well-endowed, but instead the situations in which he sets his nude figures. His *Theseus and Perithous at the Chutes* places two completely nude men at a rodeo, where they are surrounded by fully clothed men. In his *Hercules Dressing for the Arena,* Hercules is painted completely naked, except for a cowboy hat, with a rope slung over one shoulder. Because the two nudes in *Theseus and Perithous at the Chutes* are contemporary renderings of a classical ideal, their nudity is justified, even expected.[8] Their bodies are certainly worthy of the Greek comparison, except for the body hair and their large penises, which would look ridiculous and out of place on a Greek statue.

It has been suggested that the male body in art is used to showcase the workings of that body and not how that body looks.[9] This may or may not have been true of the art of ancient Greece, and it could explain Michelangelo's and Leonardo's scientific interest in the workings of male musculature. However, such a statement cannot apply to the male nude in twentieth-century art. How the body works is of little concern to artists or to those who view art. It is without question the *appearance* of the male body that is the emphasis in twentieth-century art using the male body as its subject. Few of us will look at these pieces of art and wonder about the workings of the male bodies we see.

PICTURE THIS

As with other artistic expressions, it has become difficult for us to look at a photograph of a nude man and see him as anything but a photographer's concept of ideal beauty and a societal representation of the ultimate sex partner. Certainly there is a difference in reactions when we look at, for example, a photograph done by Ansel Adams and one done by Bruce Weber, Herb Ritts, or Tom Bianchi.

Weber, Ritts, and Bianchi are probably the most renowned of the contemporary photographers of the nude male. Certainly there are others who take or took pictures of nude men, but few come near the commercial success of these three. Walk into almost any greeting card or gift store and you will find rack after rack of mass-produced cards and calendars printed with Weber, Ritts, and Bianchi photographs.

One writer, discussing the male nude in photography, argues that modern-day photographic representations of the male body do not reflect historical images because, for one reason, modern men are depicted with ample amounts of body hair.[10] What hair? The bodies used in photographs by today's commercially successful photographers would fit quite nicely on a pedestal and stand perfectly beside a *kouros* from the fifth century B.C.

The models being used in modern photography, at least in commercial photography, reflect images of male beauty that dominate modern society. It has gone on for too long to be called a trend. The body types of men used in today's commercialized photographs are white, hairless (either naturally so or shaved), and always muscular. If the faces are shown, they are ones that could only be called handsome, good-looking, or beautiful.

These soft-core—often hard-core—pictures are marketed and sold as art but are really propaganda. Here, as in the propaganda art of Nazi Germany, art is used to entice and trick our minds into believing that what we see is the truth. If it is good propaganda, the more we see and hear something espoused as the truth, the more we believe it to be true. Ask the millions of women who are expected to live up to truths they did not create or define.

Photographers of the nude male might just as well use one body, since they all are glaringly, blatantly similar. Although one model may have muscles that are larger than those of another model, the message to the viewer/buyer is the same: Here is the type of man with whom you *really* want to have sex. If you are having sex with men who do not look like this, then you are not *really* having sex. Modern culture, art included, leaves no room for personal taste or individual desire.

Photographers interested in making money from their work know that to be commercially successful their work will, in some way, need to involve the naked body. Certainly there is a market for photographs of the female nude. However, in photographing and selling the female nude photographers run the risk of being labeled sexist and, more than likely, will be accused of promoting the female body as nothing more than a brainless sex object. The photographs found in *Playboy, Penthouse,* or any of the other men's magazines are only photographs, in reality, but they can be justified simply by calling them art. Yet they are photographs that cause a great deal of controversy because they are included in magazines which are essentially about sex. It is not the photographs themselves causing so much trouble; it is what they are alleged to stand for or showcase that becomes controversial. They are accused of promoting misogyny, rape, and other acts of violence against women. They are thought to debase all women. They are believed to create false or exaggerated images of female sexuality and female appearance. Many argue that women are damaged and degraded by these kinds of photographs.

Yet few have come along to say that men are equally harmed by similar photographs in similar magazines. Few, male or female, are crying out about what the photographs of naked men may be doing to the self-esteem and self-worth of men. A depiction of men as sex objects damages and degrades men in exactly the same way as the female counterparts damage and degrade women. Men's bodies are placed in the same position as women's bodies, as objects of desire and as examples of an ideal. If this is considered harmful to women, it should be considered equally harmful to men.

IN DEFENSE OF STEREOTYPES

If in contemporary photography of the male nude there were not the projection of idealized male beauty, there would be, then, no need to defend or criticize the use of male nudity in this medium. Apparently, though, the need does exist. Otherwise, there would be no need for *In Defense of Beauty*, written by photographer Tom Bianchi.

Bianchi admits to being accused of photographing only beautiful men. In defense, Bianchi reverses the accusation and places blame on the viewer, who becomes the one misunderstanding *his* concept of accepted beauty. Because of this misunderstanding, Bianchi believes, we lessen ourselves and "trivialize" beauty.[11]

The fault, however, is not in beauty itself but rather in how beauty is used and how a type or definition of beauty is espoused as the ideal of universal, objective beauty. Bianchi's photographs are *his* concept of what makes a man beautiful. The fault of his photographs is that they are no different from the photographs of his contemporaries, such as Weber and Ritts. By duplicating what is already commonly accepted as a standard of male beauty, it is Bianchi who trivializes beauty. He is not offering something new or a different, more objective definition of male beauty. What is negative is Bianchi's continued depiction of one body type as the reigning example of male beauty. So too is his continued display of these male objects as physical role models for gay men. Why should men, gay or straight, aspire to become *someone else's* image of beauty? This leaves little room for individual expression of what is and what is not beautiful, and it puts many in a place where they often feel isolated and set apart from the rest.

Bianchi argues that the unbeautiful must first see what is considered beautiful before they can express beauty or become beautiful in their own right. This scenario creates a situation in which one is not *learning* what is beautiful but rather is being *told* what is beautiful. It presents a question with only a single answer—the male bodies in Bianchi's photographs. Why should the viewer conform to the photographer's opinion? Is this the role of art and of artists in our society?

In one telling passage of his book, Bianchi quotes a writer who obviously feels less than equal to the men in Bianchi's photographs. The writer wishes Bianchi could find beauty in "ordinary mortals."[12] Clearly, by viewing the men in Bianchi's work, this writer is made to feel physically insignificant, particularly if the men in the photographs are the gauges against which the standards of male beauty are measured. In expressing his desire for Bianchi to seek and photograph what is beautiful in men not found in Bianchi's work, a clear distinction is made between the gods in the photographs and the mortals of everyday life. An upper and lower echelon of existence is established; the criteria of both are blatantly explained and espoused as a version of someone's truth, in this case, Bianchi's truth.

In relating a story of how he and his partner came to choose a man, or rather a body, for one of his photography sessions, Bianchi tells of the model's seclusion in his Fire Island beach house. As Bianchi tells us, it was the man's discomfort with his "weight problem" that kept him inside. Bianchi was unable to accept that the man ever had a weight problem until he was shown photographs of the man before the weight loss occurred. Needless to say, Bianchi saw fit to include only the after pictures in one of his later books.[13] Bianchi could not publish the "before" photographs because they in no way represent Bianchi's ideal of male beauty. In Bianchi's mind, there is nothing extraordinary about a man who is overweight.

In an attempt to dispel the notion or suggestion that he only photographs muscular subjects, Bianchi does on occasion photograph men in their forties and fifties. However, it is obvious in examining these photographs that the men were chosen and included not because of their ages but because of the appearance of their bodies. In these photographs, Bianchi continues to depict well-built boys because the shape and size of the bodies of these older men are the same as those of boys or younger men. Their age is only apparent in their faces. They are extraordinary older men because of their beautiful bodies. Without the beautiful bodies, they would be simply older men and would not have been photographed.

In his book, Bianchi draws a correlation between a beautiful body and a satisfactory relationship. He tells the story of a man who, after the end of a relationship, decides to change his physical appearance.[14] Although it is not clear why this young man's relationship ended, the implication is there, at least in part, that it had something to do with the way he looked physically. The demise of the relationship suddenly made the man evaluate how he looked, suggesting that perhaps an improvement in his physical appearance would bring about an equal improvement in the longevity of his personal relationships with other men.

Further in his book, Bianchi argues that we are able to bring beauty into our own lives only *after* we have allowed ourselves to escape from the "bondage" of our insecurities.[15] Although it is true that an overweight or otherwise unsatisfactory body may produce insecurity, surely it is possible for someone to overcome insecurity and remain overweight or otherwise physically unsatisfactory. Bianchi blatantly suggests that fat or skinny men, or any man who does not look like a Bianchi model, cannot possibly attract beauty or possess inner strength or beauty.

Perhaps the most disturbing aspect of Bianchi's book is his discussion on HIV and AIDS. In a very self-congratulatory tone, Bianchi tells us that within his photographs of "perfect men" are men infected with HIV or men living through various stages of AIDS. He further offers that the deaths of some of his photography subjects came quickly on the heels of their having been photographed.[16] Here, Bianchi seems relieved in some way, almost as if he were lucky to get to these men before they were physically ravished by their illnesses, which would have rendered them less than perfect.

*   *   *

The treatment of the ideal male body in art has been with us for a long time and shows no sign of waning. Sculptures and paintings from ancient Greece, the Renaissance, the twentieth century, and, especially, modern photography have initiated a starting point and provided a continuation of our concepts of ideal male beauty. The culmination and the commercialized use of these ideas has made it nearly impossible for modern men to understand and know what it means to be male in our society. Issues of masculinity, projected by the visual media as the truth, at least in physical terms, confuse more than they enlighten. Emphasis is placed on the body and how the body must look. This is the power of the male nude in visual art, illustrating without question how men should appear, leaving nothing to the imagination because the image is directly in front of us and must therefore be real. These images stare us down and intimidate us into believing that they are the gods and the rest are not.

Every artist has the right to paint, draw, sculpt, or photograph his or her individual expression of what he or she thinks is beautiful. However, when an artistic expression is touted or construed as the ideal of an entire culture, freedom of expression is seriously distorted; it is painted over and becomes something altogether different.

Chapter 3

A Real Head Turner: Fiction

Fiction gives us the opportunity to escape our real lives and the real world. We travel to cities and countries filled with wonder. We find ourselves lost in intrigue and adventure that usually exceeds the limitations of our everyday existence. We fall in and out of love. We find ourselves in and out of bed. We are introduced to people we admire, envy, and desire.

Fiction is often based on actual life events or experiences. Moreover, the characters of fiction are often based on real people. Where do writers get their inspiration for the characters they create in their writing? They do not have to look far to find ample inspiration for handsome and muscular men. Our culture is full of these male specimens and offers writers plenty of material from which to develop their male characters.

Whether we are reading about heroes in selections of classical mythology or lovers in selections of modern literature, men in these stories and writings share certain basic physical similarities. They are beautiful or handsome, and most have muscular bodies. And just as often, particularly in modern writing, they possess above-average penises.

Other than that they are widely read and written by well-known writers, the books discussed in this chapter were chosen for no particular reason. Although they are a minute sampling of literature, they do serve as evidence that stereotypes of male beauty and male physical appearance are common in fiction writing and have been for quite some time.

The physical descriptions of male characters in fiction are not restricted to one particular genre. We expect to find attractive men in romance fiction. Otherwise, we would not have had to experience the Fabio phenomenon, and the cover illustrations for these novels would be quite different from what they are.

Outside the romance genre, male stereotypes are everywhere in fiction. Whether we are reading books about farm families in the Midwest, vampires and ghosts, action/adventure heroes, or gay track stars, there are few differences in the physical makeup of these male bodies. They all deliver the same message: only attractive and well-built, and often well-hung, men are worthy of having love affairs within the pages of a novel. These men are the only ones we, the readers, are allowed to fantasize about and desire.

MYTHS AND LEGENDS

In classical mythology, the hero is the one who battles and conquers monsters, other men, sometimes women, and often gods. The hero of mythology, because he is always one of the beautiful and good, inevitably gets the girl or the god of his dreams. Sometimes, too, the hero is a male god who lusts and longs for a mortal girl or woman or boy or man.

In the classical story of Cupid and Psyche, the reader has the advantage of knowing about Cupid's beauty. Psyche does not possess this knowledge, and this becomes a crucial element of the story. All Psyche has is the love for someone she has never seen. As it turns out, however, love is not enough. "What did she really know about [Cupid]?" Psyche asks herself. "If he was not horrible to look at, then he was cruel to forbid her ever to behold him." In other words, if he was beautiful, how unfair it was of him not to let her see his beauty and revel in it. It does not matter that Psyche already loves Cupid without ever having seen him. Love means nothing if the beloved is not lovely to behold. "There must be something very wrong for him to shun the light of day." Only the ugly would hide their faces from the light of the sun. Psyche is convinced that her beloved is a horrible creature. It isn't until she brings a lamp to his bed while he sleeps that she sees finally that he is attractive, snuffing out her horrible fears.[1]

Upon being seen by Psyche, Cupid flees, but not before he imparts his important message: "Love," he says, "cannot live where there is no trust."[2]

Resplendent physical beauty and great physical strength are mainstays of classical mythology and of the heroes and lovers who appear in the stories. Pyramus was "the most beautiful youth," Theseus was a man who possessed "great bodily strength," and Hercules, perhaps the greatest hero of them all, had the "supreme self-confidence magnificent physical strength gives."[3]

In addition to myths, other historical writings pay homage to physical beauty. In Plato's *Symposium*, for example, we read, "Love set in order the empire of the gods—the love of beauty, as is evident, for of deformity there is no love" and ". . . from the love of the beautiful, has sprung every good in heaven and earth."[4] The ugly, it seems, are damned.

ROMANCING THE BODY

Romance fiction would not exist, and certainly would not comprise an estimated 46 percent of the pocket book market, without handsome, strong, and often well-endowed men. Would there be 50 million romance readers around the world without such men?[5]

Few, if any, want to read love stories that have ugly, weak, or less-endowed men as principal characters. Because romance, both in writing and real life, is so closely associated with sex, it is imperative that romance novels have within their pages a cast of characters who are sexually appealing to one another and to the reader.

In the first few pages of Susannah Leigh's *Dawn Shadows,* we find Maria swimming in a pool of water in a Hawaiian jungle. After a few moments, Maria realizes she is being watched by a man. She is about to verbally condemn her onlooker but stops when she gets a good look at him. What did she see that made her change her mind?

In the next paragraph, we are told that the man watching Maria had ". . . muscles that seemed to ripple across his chest" and that the "way he held his head" seemed to signal to Maria that this man was ". . . not a mere mortal at all but something different." In other words, he was a god.[6]

By the end of the first chapter, on page 28, Maria and Sandy have made love three times. This is quite a change of heart, given that when she first noticed him spying on her in the pool she "raised her eyes to meet his with a flash of righteous indignation." We can be certain that if Sandy did not possess the physical qualities that made him so beautiful, so attractive, there would have been no lovemaking between him and Maria.[7]

"He was good-looking," we are told on page 47 of Danielle Steel's *The Gift*. "It was impossible not to notice how handsome he was," we read on page 52. By page 55, he is "looking incredibly handsome." On page 59, he becomes ". . . so unbelievably handsome." Finally, on page 134, we are introduced to his ". . . powerful arms and legs."[8]

Writers of romance fiction often let readers know immediately what type of men await them in the pages that follow. For example, here is the opening line of Judith McNaught's *Until You:* "Propped upon a mountain of satin pillows amid rumpled bed linens, Helen Devernay surveyed his bronzed, muscular torso with an appreciative smile."[9]

Readers of romance fiction want fantasies about men who are drop-dead gorgeous and who have rippling muscles. They do not want fantasies about men who are ugly or plain or fat or skinny. The implication is that ugly, plain, fat, or skinny men are too much a part of the real world, and no one, it seems, can love or fantasize about these types of men.

BEST-SELLING BODIES

Male beauty and muscularity are not relegated to the pages of romance fiction. Best-selling books falling within other genres of writing are equally exacting in the depictions of the male body. In Jane Smiley's best-selling novel *A Thousand Acres*, we learn early in the story that Jess is someone to behold, with ". . . muscles inside his jeans."[10]

Nearly halfway through *A Thousand Acres*, we learn that Ty, the protagonist's husband, has "wide and muscular" shoulders. Later, we have the protagonist more fully describing Jess, who has by now become her lover: "I think of his abdomen and arms and back and shoulder muscles, present in every man . . . like some sort of virtue."[11]

In the best-selling book, *The Bridges of Madison County,* Francesca watches Robert Kincaid walk toward her: "[S]he could see tight chest muscles." Later in the novel, Kincaid is described as "[a] graceful, hard, male animal."[12]

Neither *A Thousand Acres* nor *The Bridges of Madison County* can rightfully be called romance novels, at least not in the same way as *Dawn Shadows, The Gift,* or *Until You.* These books appeal to different readers and further serve as fodder for the debate over the difference between fiction and literature. This debate aside, however, the depictions of the male characters in these books share many of the same physical qualities. Moreover, these books share one crucial element of plot—a romantic interest between two central characters. Because romance is so intricately mixed with sex, and because sexual interest between two people is so often dependent upon physical appearance, physical descriptions of male characters need not be different in romance fiction from ones in so-called literary fiction. Sandy's body in *Dawn Shadows* is interchangeable with Robert's body in *The Bridges of Madison County.* These two books may be polar opposites in the eyes of critics; however, the male characters, at least in their physical attributes, are not.

Fiction also has its share of action/adventure/thriller stories, and if sales of these books are any indication, within these stories are the fictional heroes real-life men seem to want to identify with or emulate. *Publishers Weekly* reports that more than 13 million books in this genre are sold annually.[13] Few men can identify with or wish to become these literary heroes without identifying with or wishing to possess the type of body or physical appearance of these heroes.

Action/adventure/thriller books are stories of power, control, and violence—the very same elements of our society that men currently find themselves embroiled in, pursuing, accused of possessing, or denying. Although the reality of this may remain debatable in real life, there is no question that the reality exists in men's fiction. As a publishing executive states, "[M]en's action-adventure fiction involves characters and settings that are paramilitary, guerrilla, survivalist."[14] For male fictional characters to succeed within these he-man plots—solely for the benefit of the reader—they must meet very strict physical criteria. Otherwise, they would fail as literary heroes.

Tom Clancy is one of the most commercially successful authors in this genre; his books are full of men whose physical descriptions and he-man lifestyles serve as instructions on how to be real men. Take for example the character named The Archer in Clancy's *The Cardinal of the Kremlin.* "On those occasions that he had both the desire and opportunity to bathe . . . anyone could see the youthful muscles on his thirty-year-old body."[15] It should be noted that this quote is taken from the first sentence of the novel, making it very clear to the reader that the main character is worthy of our immediate admiration and attention.

Using the legal profession as the setting for his books, John Grisham has become a dominating force in commercial fiction. Similar to Clancy's, Grisham's stories have appeared on the big screen, adding a further dimension to the exposition of the male bodies Grisham creates on paper.

Within the first 158 pages of Grisham's best-selling book, *The Firm*, there are six different references to the appearance of the male characters. The second sentence on page one of the novel sets the tone: "He has the brains, the ambition, and the good looks."[16]

Perhaps the most well-known male fictional character is James Bond. Similar to the Marlboro Man in advertising, Bond has remained a constant symbol of maleness and masculinity. For years, he has been a fantasy figure, both for women and for men. Few, if any, other male literary characters have sustained such a place in our society. Still fewer can claim to be such a powerful role model.

If in a 1963 *New York Times Magazine* article, when one young Bond fan believed that "Bond held forth the promise—that brains as well as brawn could work for you in the wider world," is it not arguable that today's young (and older) Bond fans might feel the same way? No man wants to be the scrawny intellectual in glasses. Although Bond may have intelligence, it is not his brains the Bond girls are after. Without the brawn—easily and obviously translated into muscles and good looks—his legacy and his continuing role as hero and fantasy figure would have died a long time ago.[17]

Some works of fiction are not as easily categorized as others. The works of Anne Rice are good examples of fiction that are difficult to label as belonging to a specific or single genre. Because the elements and characters of Rice's stories are so often super- or preter-natural, while including earthbound settings and mortal people, Rice's books satisfy the requirements of several different genres.

What is interesting and relevant for the sake of this discussion is Rice's treatment of her male characters' physical attributes. It doesn't matter whether a male character in one of Rice's books is a human, vampire, spirit, or new species of man. The majority of Rice's central male characters are good-looking, possess well-built bodies, and quite often come equipped with extra large penises.

In the early volumes of Rice's vampire chronicles, the handsomeness of the two leading male vampires, Lestat and Louis, exists not so much because they are meant to be objects of romantic or sexual desire (though this is what they end up being before their vampire nature is discovered by anyone desiring them) but because their good looks are holdovers from previous human existences. In other words, they were good-looking men before they became good-looking vampires. According to Rice's theory, what mortal men look like at the moment they become vampires is what they will look like for the duration of their vampire lives. What is most important to Lestat and Louis, as vampires, is their charm and irresistibility. Certainly good looks can add to a man's or a vampire's charisma and allure, and these qualities benefit Lestat and Louis because they attract victims.

Rowan, the enduring heroine of Rice's saga, *The Witching Hour* clearly enjoys a muscular male body. When Rowan meets, falls in love with, and has sex with Michael, she gets what she wants: ". . . this hard chest . . . and his thick cock . . . and the hard belly. . . . She loved the feel of these strong thighs under her fingers." Later in the book, Rowan sums up Michael's physical appearance as "Walking porn."[18]

Near the end of *The Witching Hour,* the spirit Lasher finally achieves a successful fusion with a human, resulting in the birth of a Taltos. A more complete retelling of this scene is presented in *Lasher*, the second volume of the series. As Rowan touches the Taltos for the first time, she comments that Lasher feels like a newly born child, "except that the musculature was there." A few pages later, Rowan and Lasher are in a bathtub. As Lasher, on his hands and knees above Rowan, makes his move toward sexual intercourse with Rowan, she notices "his cock was thick and slightly curved."[19] This comment is not only an appeal to the fantasies and myths of penis size but also a reminder to the reader that Lasher's penis is "perfect."[20]

In her witch series, Rice thoroughly celebrates the benefits of superior male beauty and large penises. In her vampire chronicles she makes it clear that vampires must be attractive enough to charm the pants off a would-be meal. What, then, does she do within the pages of a story about an ancient Egyptian mummy? In reading *The*

Mummy, it quickly becomes apparent that ancient relics of maleness must be attractive, like vampires, and well-built, like the Taltos.

After Ramses, the 3,000-year-old mummy, has come to life, he begins removing the bandages covering his body. In doing so, he exposes to Julie, the story's female protagonist, and to the reader, his "broad naked chest" and "powerful arms." As ". . . this beautiful man with the splendid body" comes toward Julie, she becomes confused and enthralled. It doesn't take long for Julie to realize, though, that Ramses is "the most beautiful man" she has ever seen.[21]

Julie and Ramses are not the only characters having sex in *The Mummy.* When Cleopatra is brought back to life, she too has her share of orgasmic wonders. Even though she is thousands of years old, she becomes very quickly a discerning woman of the twentieth century. When Lord Summerfield and Cleopatra are in a hotel room, Cleopatra thinks, "Oh, he was so much sweeter than all the others, and when a strong man is sweet, even goddesses look down from Mount Olympus."[22] In other words, the goddesses who reside on Mount Olympus do not bother to look at men who are not strong and sweet. Rice attempts to make this discriminatory observation peculiar only to goddesses who inhabit Mount Olympus. In reality, however, she is merely invoking identical discriminatory observations made by more than a few twentieth-century, earthbound, mortal women.

PINK PAGES

In literature aimed at a gay male readership, it is almost always a certainty that the dominant male characters are beautiful and muscular. Writers of books for and about gay men rely heavily on physical attributes of their male characters. Almost without fail, the descriptions of good-looking and muscular men fill the pages of most novels and stories written about gay men and their love lives.

Maurice, the title character of E. M. Forster's 1914 novel, is described as being "attractive and beautiful." Further into the novel, it becomes apparent that Maurice expects his admirers to be equally good-looking. While riding on a train one day, Maurice is sharing a compartment with another man: "This person, stout and greasy-faced, made a lascivious sign, and, off his guard, Maurice responded. Next moment both rose to their feet. The other man smiled, whereupon Maurice knocked him down. . . . Maurice stood over him, black-browed, and saw in this disgusting and dishonorable old age his own."[23] With what we know of Maurice by this point in the novel, it is clear that had the man been young and handsome Maurice's reaction would have been to throw a kiss instead of a punch.

Oscar Moore's *A Matter of Life and Sex* is, in part, the coming-out/coming-of-age story of Hugo. As a young boy coping with thoughts of homosexuality, Hugo dreams of being with ". . . muscular creatures whose hairless bodies flexed beautifully." Hugo gets erections during his daily rides on a school bus and ponders the cause, determining that the unruly erections were caused by the sweaty and shirtless construction workers he saw on the street. As a school-age boy, Hugo already knows it is muscles that make a man attractive and sexy. Later in the novel, Hugo learns just how important muscles are in gay male sex, particularly to men who are willing to pay for sex with another man: ". . . Hugo didn't have the muscles he was looking for. Muscles were in and they were ruining Hugo's business."[24]

A Matter of Life and Sex also speaks very loudly about the role of older men in gay male culture. When Hugo learns of the abundant availability of gay male sex in public bathrooms, he also discovers evidence that older men are not tolerated and are not wanted. Written on the bathroom walls were "[a]ngry messages moaning about the old men who loitered unwanted in the corner, staring and winking, spurned without remorse." Hugo's thoughts of older men were mixed, though no less discriminating than the bathroom authors. He liked to be watched while masturbating in the public bathroom: "Even if it was the despised old men he wouldn't let touch him."[25] Old men are allowed to watch, but a line is drawn when it comes to touching.

Published in the 1970s, Patricia Nell Warren's *The Front Runner* continues to sell in gay male culture. It teaches gay men, young and old, what it takes to be an attractive, desirable gay man.

The Front Runner uses the world of running to glorify the athlete's body. In assessing his own sexual desires, Harlan, the running coach and the novel's narrator, has this thought while looking for sex in the bars of New York City: "[L]ooking athletic is as important as being well hung. . . . The sad thing was . . . that so few of my bed partners were real athletes"—and, presumably, not satisfying bed partners—"I learned fast not to waste my tenderness on them."[26] Tenderness, it seems, can only be given to men who have athletic bodies.

As for the other male characters in *The Front Runner*, Vince was "the best-looking" of the three runners. Jacques "was a shade more muscular than Vince." The stranger Harlan has sex with in the theatre was "lean and hard-looking." There is Denny who "would have caused a riot on Sheridan Square." John, Billy's father, was "more muscular [than Billy]."[27]

More than a novel filled with sexy, beautiful men, *The Front Runner* is also a kind of how-to manual on assessing suitable and satisfying sexual partners. The novel unabashedly states that the ultimate gay male sex partner is a man who has a muscular body: "A man's body is good to look at only when he is conditioned, because of the muscling."[28]

In *Harlan's Race*, the sequel to *The Front Runner*, the beauty goes on. In a Montreal hotel room, shortly after Billy has been assassinated in the Olympic Games, Harlan is surrounded by beautiful men. Vince's face, though tearstained, was still "handsome," while Harry had "the . . . good looks of a blond Rock Hudson."[29]

Later in the book, two bodyguards find themselves staring at "Vince's magnificent crotch." Harlan, at the age of forty-two, is still attractive, seeming to transcend the gay stereotype that growing old means growing ugly. In the narrative, he says that he was "[f]lat-muscled as a young man," and at forty-two, he "was . . . 'ripped.'" Even a pet cat is turned into a sex object, having "balls as big as his paws."[30]

The dance floor of a bar on Fire Island was crowded with "Beautiful People" (notice the capitalizations). While he watches Vince dance, Harlan remembers how Billy's life was cut short and suddenly imagines the same happening to Vince at the bar. If a bullet went through Vince, as it had with Billy, it would destroy "that perfect body." A bullet destroys the body before it kills the person. Finally, Harlan approaches Vince on the dance floor and drags away "the reigning beauty." Harlan takes Vince home, and they get into the shower together. Here Harlan feels Vince's "magnificent limp cock" resting against him.[31]

As they play naked in the ocean, Harlan puts his arms around Vince and lifts him into the air. While holding Vince's buttocks, Harlan describes them as being "hard as rounded rocks."[32]

Vince's remarkable buttocks are mentioned again on page 249. While running one day, after Harlan and Vince finally come together as a couple, Harlan tells us that he "reached over and smacked [Vince] on his hard butt. [Vince] smacked me on my hard butt."[33] Finally, the two hard butts are together, rightfully deserving of their mutual and complementary physical beauty.

BEDTIME BODIES

While adult men and women who read about other adult men and women are learning about satisfying love and sex partners in their novels, what are children learning in their books and stories? As it turns out, children are learning the same lessons. Sleeping Beauty is awakened by a kiss from a handsome prince. A frog is turned into a handsome prince when allowed to sleep for three nights under a beautiful princess's pillow. Cinderella is changed forever into a beautiful princess only when the equally beautiful prince comes along and matches the slipper to her foot.

One of the most famous children's stories is *Beauty and the Beast*. The story of Beauty and the Beast is very similar to the story of Cupid and Psyche. Unlike Psyche, however, Beauty knows the Beast is a monster. Whereas the lesson in the story of Cupid and Psyche is one of trust, the presumed lesson in *Beauty and the Beast* is to look beyond what is on the surface to what lies beneath.

There are many versions of this classic fairy tale, each of them differing only slightly in plot, character, and dialogue. In most versions, we are eventually offered the explanation that the Beast is turned into a beast because of his refusal to help an old woman who appears at his castle door one day. He is cursed with ugliness and forced to live as a monster until the day when someone can learn to love him despite his horrible and hideous looks. This is a not-so-subtle lesson or message that ugly equals bad. The ultimate punishment for a refusal of help is to be transformed into an ugly being, with a life of bitter loneliness.

To break the curse, the Beast must win the love of a woman, despite his physical appearance. Over time, Beauty makes this possible, finally seeing through the Beast's horrible appearance and discovering the true beauty living in his heart. This would be the perfect place to end this story and would bring *Beauty and the Beast* into the realm of a myth, one showing us how to overcome our cultural emphasis on outward appearance. Unfortunately, the story continues.

In all of the versions of *Beauty and the Beast,* the ending is the same. Beauty at last finds the true love she wants. By looking beyond the Beast's ugliness, she becomes one of the few human beings who experiences true love. Because Beauty has been so patient, so understanding in her journey of love's triumph over the obstacle of ugliness, the Beast is transformed into a handsome prince. "Come and receive the reward of your noble choice. You preferred virtue to beauty and wit and you surely deserve to find all these qualities in one person."[34]

How sad it is, particularly given how long it has been around, that the story of *Beauty and the Beast* has not escaped our culture's insistence that being beautiful is better than being ugly. To be beautiful is a reward. To be ugly is a curse. These are the points stressed in *Beauty and the Beast.* Surely there are more important facts of life that can be explained and taught to children through literature.

* * *

Whether it is Francesca admiring Robert's chest or Helen Devernay surveying her lover's body or Vince's and Harlan's coupled anatomical perfection running side by side on the beach, the stereotyped male body—handsome, muscular—dominates fiction.

There are no doubt thousands upon thousands of other books containing descriptions of beautiful men within their pages. These men are making female and gay male readers weak in the knees and straight male readers envious. The fantasies—ones of ultimate sex, happiness, satisfaction, and partnerships—are forming in the minds of millions of readers. Perfect love and lovers are ours as we ride the subway or bus to work or read at night as we try to fall asleep. Perfect sex could be ours if only the man in bed next to us looked a little bit more like Sandy, Mark, Lucas, Jess, Ty, Robert, Michael, Lasher, Maurice, Vince, Jacques, Billy, Harlan, a 3,000-year-old mummy, or even Horatio the cat.

Chapter 4

Buy Me: Advertising

The purpose of advertising is to sell a product to as many consumers as possible. To do this successfully, the advertiser (or advertising agency) takes a particular product and puts it before the public eye in an attractive and appealing package. There was a time when a car company wanting to sell a car was able to do so by showing a photograph of the car. Once, a clothing manufacturer could sell a line of blue jeans by showing a photograph of the jeans. Those times are gone now, seemingly forever.

Sometime during the course of advertising evolution, manufacturers and advertisers realized that the product alone was not enough to grab the consumer's attention. It was not enough that a car be a car or that a pair of blue jeans be a pair of blue jeans. These are products, mere things. With the advent of rampant consumerism in the 1980s, selling a product became a cutthroat business, making it necessary for manufacturers and advertising agencies to create new selling schemes and devices.

Advertisers had long known that one surefire way to sell a product was by marrying the product with something everyone, or almost everyone, thought of and wanted—sex. Because advertising was then, and is today, a heterosexual male–dominated industry, sex was equated with women. Women became spokespersons for everything from car companies to airlines. Advertisers took women out of the kitchen, momentarily, and, in a way, put them in the bedroom.

Advertising is about image and image enhancement. A car can have an image of its own, but enhance the image with a beautiful and shapely woman, and you have a product more people, men in particular, will want to buy. "Advertising . . . knows the worth of things that catch and enchant the eye."[1] What better way to do this than by showing beautiful, idealized women who, in turn, become the idealized and fantasized sex partners of men.

Most of us know what happened when women's bodies started popping up in advertisements. Feminists cried foul. Yet advertisers argued that they were giving society only what society wanted, since "[a]dvertising doesn't lead society, it follows."[2] Advertising became part of Naomi Wolf's "beauty myth" and Susan Faludi's "backlash," images of women that did irreparable damage to women's self-esteem and self-confidence. Women were stereotyped and objectified, projected as ideals of femininity, material for many a man's sexual fantasy.

By the 1980s, the women's movement was in full swing and was able, to some extent, to change how women were depicted in advertising. Women and their bodies were as present as ever in advertising, but the blatant sexism had lessened; or rather became less blatant and more subtle and subliminal. The female flight attendant's "Fly me" was gone, but her body, in all of its stereotyped glory and beauty, remained. She did not have to say, "Fly me." One look at her and we knew what she was thinking and what we were supposed to be thinking in return.

If a wave of feminism in the form of a women's movement changed society's perception of women, it also changed society's perception of men. Feminists not only demanded a different sort of depiction of women in advertising and the media; they demanded a different way of being treated by men. A new definition of femininity and femaleness resulted. A new woman was born, and only a new man could successfully and effectively interact with her. Women wanted these new men to change their attitudes; the definition of masculinity and maleness had to change. Women wanted men to be more than providers. If equal status was to be accorded to women, men would have to all but abandon past notions of manliness and masculinity. It was no longer enough for men to have high-paying jobs or a power seat in the corporate world. Women eschewed traditional male roles and stereotypes, and the rest of society soon followed. The advertising industry certainly did. Although an article in *Marketing* magazine on men in advertising agrees that there has been a disappearance of the traditional male stereotype in advertising, it also claims there has been nothing new to take its place.[3] A close examination of the depiction of men in current advertising, however, reveals this to be untrue.

The birth of the new man created a frenzy in the advertising world. As women's roles have changed over the years so, by extension, have men's.[4] Suddenly men were shopping for themselves, no longer relying on the women in their lives to pick out their shirts and underwear. Men became aware of the sensitivity of their skin and were beginning to be told that their skin is different from women's skin and needs to be treated accordingly, with products designed exclusively for men. Men's hair needed more than just shampoo; it needed conditioner, mousse, and gel. Men didn't need to learn this on their own, or from their lovers, girlfriends, or spouses; the advertising industry was there to tell them. The way men look started to change in very dramatic ways. Subsequently, their physical appearance needed to change into something considered more suitable, something more sexually desirable.[5] What is better suited than the advertising industry to promote this new brand of male sexual desirability?

If men are to be sex objects, what must they look like? What is this new image of men that advertising has given us? During the 1980s, male models became thinner, and the suits they wore were designed to enhance that thinness.[6] Slimness and clothes that accentuate the body, once worries and expectations assigned to women, became important criteria of male image that launched an advertising phenomenon which in the end, would stereotype men in exactly the same way women have been stereotyped.

Print advertisements found in numerous magazines and newspapers tell men and women—sometimes blatantly, sometimes subtly—how men must present themselves, how men must take care of themselves, what men must own, how men must live, what men must smell like, and what it is that defines male sexuality. The most obvious message given in print advertisements, however, is what men must look like to be considered one of the new men, worthy of the latest definitions of masculinity and maleness.

Examination of advertisements using male bodies to sell products reveals that there is more than products being sold. Whether or not this is the intent of the advertising industry is not the point. The point is that viewers, the consumers, see particular images of men becoming the standard of male physical attractiveness to which they compare themselves or other men. If viewers/consumers are male, they are left to wonder why they do not look like the men in advertisements. If viewers/consumers are female or gay men, they are left to wonder why their mates or the men they date and/or have sex with do not look like the men in advertisements.

THE SMELL OF IT

Certain products lend themselves well to naked male bodies in print advertisements. Cologne ads, for example, are mainly photographs of muscled men. Most of these advertisements show naked male torsos with sculpted stomach and chest muscles; some use photographs of handsome faces and penetrating eyes glaring at the reader, seeming to say: "Do you look like this?" or "Don't you wish you looked like me?"

Cologne ads are featured regularly in men's magazines. In some cases, they do more than show a man's body and a bottle of cologne—they tell us a story. An advertisement for Fabergé's Brut Actif Blue is a series of photographs depicting a man going kayaking. First we see him shirtless, carrying his kayak. Then we see photographs of him fighting and conquering the rapids, while a beautiful woman watches from the banks of the river. In the end, we see the man embracing the woman as if she were his reward for defeating the water. "The essence of man," the copy reads.

Male nudity has become a prominent, almost necessary, component in advertisements for men's cologne. These ad campaigns have played a significant role in promoting an image of the ideal male body. Advertisements for Calvin Klein's cologne are perhaps the most well-known ads of this kind. The ad campaign for Klein's Obsession cologne is thought to be "[t]he campaign most often pointed to as pushing new boundaries for the male image, . . . with sculpted, almost nude, bodies."[7] Regardless of who started the trend of male nudity in advertising, other cologne manufacturers and their advertisers quickly followed suit. Although advertisements for different colognes vary in location and setting, there is little variation in the type of male bodies being used or in the degree of nudity. It is not often that we find a cologne advertisement which does not, in some way, show a naked male body.

In advertisements for women's cologne, near-naked male bodies are often prominently displayed. For example, a women's cologne called Caesar's Woman shows a man with only a cloth wrapped around his waist, his chest and stomach muscles prominently displayed. The copy reads, "The most sensuous fragrance since Caesar perfected pleasure." Notice how perfected pleasure is attributed to a man.

The photographs in cologne advertisements speak for themselves in terms of promoting an ideal male physique. But in case we do not comprehend visually, the advertisements give us written copy that is always suggestive and is nearly always blatant in its attempt to brainwash consumers.

A brand of cologne called 4711 uses the phrase, "It feels unreal," with a photograph of a naked man being splashed by water. To most of us looking at this particular advertisement it is probably the man who feels, or at least seems, more "unreal" than the cologne.[8] An advertisement for Paco Rabanne's XS cologne says that the cologne provides "sensation to excess." This point is illustrated by showing a man's body from just above the pectoral area to the top of his pants. The bottle of cologne rests on his stomach, just above his belt. He grasps the phallic-shaped bottle in a way that can only suggest masturbation. A cologne called Gravity is said to be "more than a fragrance, it's a force of a nature." Stetson cologne is "easy to wear" and "hard to resist." Jovan's Musk for Men asks, "What attracts?" Avon's Triumph is "what every man wants" and "what every woman wants him to have."

In their ongoing effort to explain the complicated workings of male-female relationships, men's magazines sometimes feature articles on men's cologne. These articles sometimes focus on whether women consider smell when choosing or looking for male partners.

An article in *Gentlemen's Quarterly* titled "Scent of a Man" asks, "Will wearing the right fragrance make women want to have sex with you?" The article is less than interesting, but the photograph used to illustrate the article certainly is titillating. In the photograph, a man is completely naked as he stands at a bar. The two women who sit on either side of him are fully dressed. A first glance at this photograph reveals an obvious attempt at reverse sexism—two dressed women ogling a naked man. A closer examination, however, shows that this is not the case at all. The absurdity of a naked man standing in a bar with two fully dressed women is completely glossed over. By virtue of his nakedness between two fully dressed women, the man is intended to be the object of desire. His nakedness in a bar—a setting no doubt purposely chosen because of its pick-up reputation—attempts to make him the game and the two women the hunters. The intent to place the man as the object of desire and the attempt to position him as the hunted fail, however, because of body positions and facial expressions.

The man stands at the bar, between the two sitting women. The positioning of these three bodies makes it necessary for the two women to look *up* to the man. The man stares into the camera, while one of the women stares at his profile and the other woman stares at the back of his head. The two facial expressions of the women alternate between a look of dreamy desire and a look of quiet desperation. The man's facial expression, however, is quite different. The smug look on his face and his masterful smile clearly place him in the superior position, despite being naked in public while the two women are fully dressed. In being admired and desired by *two* women, he is fulfilling a popular fantasy among straight men. The viewer is led to believe, or at least to imagine, that the man in the photograph is going to have sex with not one woman but two at the same time. At this point, probably few readers care about the content of the article.

What is most disturbing about this photograph, however, is that a naked man among clothed women is deemed permissible. It would not be permissible if the situation were reversed. Interesting, too, is that this particular photograph shows up in a men's magazine. Why a naked man in a men's magazine instead of a naked woman? Surely the editors of *Gentlemen's Quarterly* are not purposely putting naked men in their magazine for the enjoyment of their male readers. After all, isn't *Gentlemen's Quarterly* supposed to be a magazine for straight men? If this is so, the only explanation for the photograph would be to educate *Gentlemen's Quarterly* readers on what their bodies had better look like if they ever want to find themselves standing naked in a bar with two women looking on adoringly.[9]

Since it is not always possible to show in an advertisement how a cologne smells, advertisers have chosen instead to show what men must look like to be worthy of such smells. All of this is done, of course, in an effort to attract women. No matter how pleasant men might smell, if their bodies do not meet the criteria of today's ideal male physique, they will never find themselves the objects of a woman's desire. They certainly will not find themselves in cologne advertisements.

BRIEFING THE STEREOTYPE

Another product whose advertisements are more frequently aimed at men is underwear. There may have been a day when men wore only white boxer shorts or white briefs or whatever their wives or girlfriends or mothers bought for them. It is possible that at one time men simply didn't care about their underwear. Today, however, underwear is much more than a piece of underclothing; underwear is a consumerist symbol of masculinity just as lingerie is a consumerist symbol of femininity. Underwear is bought for and by men because it makes them look sexier, not because it is comfortable.

The marketing of men's underwear gives the advertising industry the perfect vehicle to showcase the male body. What better justification is there for using the male body as an object to sell a product? After all, every man wears underwear. However, not every man can be in underwear ads.

An advertisement in a nationally known newspaper for a department store sale on men's underwear tells readers that the store sells underwear in waist sizes twenty-eight to fifty. Along with the ad copy are several photographs of men wearing various styles of underwear. Not one of the men in the photographs has a fifty-inch waist. In fact, it appears that none of them have a waist much more than thirty or thirty-two inches.

The bodies of men in underwear ads demand our attention much quicker than the brand of underwear they happen to be wearing. Modern-day underwear ads—from Calvin Klein to Jockey to Joe Boxer—dangerously skirt the line between advertising and erotica. Quite often, the only element distinguishing the photographs of men in underwear advertisements from photographs in, for example,

Playgirl or any of the many erotic magazines for gay men, is the underwear itself. Without the underwear, the men in the advertisements would fit quite nicely in erotic photo spreads and centerfolds.

Manufacturers for a line of underwear called $2^{(x)}$ist produce a catalog pushing a line of underwear not any more interesting than or different in style or design from any other line of underwear. The catalog is not about selling underwear; it is a catalog selling a very specific type of male body. It is clear that not one of these models has a fifty-inch waist. In fact, $2^{(x)}$ist's Classic Fly-Front Brief only comes in even waist sizes, twenty-eight to thirty-eight. Everyone else is simply out of luck, dismissed.

Underwear advertisements appear to be more about sexual attraction than anything else. In truth, does it really matter what underwear looks like, since, in most everyday situations, underwear is not visible as an article of clothing? Underwear is designed to highlight certain male body parts—the buttocks and the genitals. Underwear ads are about making a man look more sexy, more desirable, and showcasing an idealized male body. Depending on the publication in which they appear, underwear ads are either discreet or blatant about the appearance of male genitals.

The only discernible difference between men's underwear advertisements in daily newspapers and *Details* or *Gentlemen's Quarterly*, for example, is that in the former the genitals are usually smoothed with, perhaps, tissue paper, in an effort to disguise their appearance. In the latter publications, as well as others, the genitals are not smoothed at all and are very visible through the material of the underwear. These ads are purposely made to be erotic and suggestive, furthering the wave of male beauty propaganda on which the advertising industry survives. We are made to believe that men are desirable only if they have bulging genitals and firm, round buttocks. The truth is, of course, that all men do not have these hyped physical traits. Those who do not are, again, dismissed as objects of sexual desirability.

GORILLA SUITS

If men want to look like the men in cologne and underwear advertisements, they must exercise their bodies and make them compatible with the advertising industry's version of the ideal male. The exercise equipment industry advertises several products that can help men achieve this goal. Ads for exercise equipment make it very clear that a tight, fit body is what every man requires to feel good and, more important, to look good: Pro-Form Cross Trainer—"Designer clothes deserve a designer body." Pro-Form Cross Walk—"Great bodies are made, not born." NordicTrack—"NordicTrack helps you look and feel your best." NordicFlex Gold—"The best choice for building a hard body." The Body Sculptor—"Develop the body you've always dreamed of having." Bowflex—"If you want a fit, lean, strong body, Bowflex is for you."

To exercise properly, men must wear the appropriate exercise clothing. The exercise world is one of body-hugging shorts and low-cut, body-exposing T-shirts. Popular exercise clothing is designed and advertised as attention-getting attire. The more body exposed, the more popular the clothing. Although it seems that exercise clothing should be made for comfort and moveability, neither of these components enter into today's lines of exercise attire for men. Look through the pages of magazines such as *Undergear, International Male*, and *Malepak,* and you will see not only what today's ideal men look like, but also what they are wearing at the gym. These catalogs offer consumers exercise clothing that is "sleek and strong" in appearance. Their clothes are "body-baring and body-conscious" and "accentuate your sculpted physique." They offer men "styles to show off every chiseled muscle" and "body-sculpting boxers and bikinis." They sell "bodywear" that is "sheer perfection." Even the names given to various lines of clothing tell men who and what they are: "body master," "body-tech," "gorilla wear."

THE APPAREL OFT PROCLAIMS THE MAN

A man's physical body is only a part of his overall image. There are other components that will either make or break a man's image. Outside the gym, a beautiful male body can be made even more beautiful with the right clothing and accessories. This must be true, since all we ever see in advertisements for men's clothing and accessories are men who are handsome and well-built.

There is the pretty boy on the cover of *DNR*, a fashion and news magazine for the men's wear industry, wearing a jacket with no shirt so we can see his highly muscled torso. There are the pouty, sensitive-looking, near-naked men in the Gianni Versace couture ads, their beautiful bodies prominently displayed whether they are indoors or outdoors. There is the shirtless man in a Valentino ad that says, "Very Valentino." We cannot be certain if the ad copy is referring to the clothes or the man. What is being sold in an advertisement for Request jeans in which a hunk of a man is lying on a bed in his underwear, grasping the neck of a champagne bottle standing between his legs? Maybe he represents what the copy in an advertisement for leather jackets says: "It's what the others wish they could be."

One possible reason why an advertiser might place a champagne bottle between a man's legs is to make an implication of desired penis size. Since no definitive answer has ever been found on whether penis size is important, and since the assumption that bigger is better continues to be the dominant thought, what man wouldn't want a penis the size of a champagne bottle? Although an exposed penis is rare in advertising, penislike images and oblique references to the penis are common. A champagne bottle is only one item used by the advertising industry as a reference to the penis. Vegetables are another. An advertisement for cigarettes uses a cucumber; another for commercial and industrial property in Maryland uses a carrot.[10]

Even the computer industry uses references to penises and penis size. A two-page ad for a multimedia computer chip shows in the first photograph a naked man with a computer monitor strategically placed in front of his genitals. The look on the man's face is one of anger and disappointment. In the center of the monitor's screen is a picture of a small fig leaf, representing the small size of the screen. Presumably, this is the reason for the man's unhappy countenance. On the page opposite, the same man is smiling and happy. Why? The fig leaf on his monitor covers the entire screen. The caption for the ad reads, "Full-motion video accelerators, yet another instance where size is everything." Since the fig leaf is famous for only one reason, there is no doubt this advertisement is telling men—and women—that penis size is something to consider. The bigger the fig leaf, the bigger the penis, the happier the man, the more satisfied the woman.

Although advertisements using men are very exact in their depiction of the ideal male body and its parts, they are not so rigid or consistent when it comes to men's ability to determine for themselves what they should and should not wear. New male stereotypes abound, but old stereotypes still have their place in modern advertising. Haggar has an ad showing a man wearing a pair of boxer shorts: "I'm damn well gonna wear what I want," the ad copy reads. Then, "Honey, what do I want?" Some men have the right body but at the same time cannot get beyond the old stereotype that they do not know or care enough about fashion to be able to pick out their own clothing. According to Haggar, choosing what men should wear continues to be the job of the wife or girlfriend. Men cannot be fashion-conscious despite their new-found role as sex symbol.

ACCESSORIES AND THEN SOME MAKE THE MAN

Once a man has the right body and the right kind of clothing to show off his body, what more does he need to be ideal? Does he need the perfect watch? There is a watch made by Franchi Menotti, advertised with a naked man and a caption that reads: "The face that launched 1,000 ships." We are supposed to believe they are talking about the face of the watch, not the face of the naked and beautiful man. Zodiac watches are "the ultimate sports watch for mere mortals." The man in the advertisement has a knife in his mouth and his hand wrapped around a snake baring its fangs. Only real men who are hunters need wear the Zodiac watch. There is the Ellesse watch, which is "designed to perform," pictured with a man clad only in bikini swimwear. If these are not enough, there is a watch made by Giorgio Beverly Hills, worn by a stunning young man. "Feel Giorgio!" the ad reads. Which is Giorgio, the watch or the man? What or who are we supposed to feel?

No matter what is being sold, men in print advertisements are predominately beautiful and muscular. We find them in ads for cigarettes: "No doubt about it," reads an ad for Kool. No doubt about what? A Kool cigarette or a cool guy? The Marlboro Man, a long-time symbol of American maleness and masculinity, is still around.

Only now he's a little younger, his face has fewer wrinkles, and he's a lot better looking than he used to be.

There are ads for videos on how straight men and straight women can spice up their sex lives: "You can reach new heights—together!" "Boost your sexual confidence." The couples photographed in these ads are always of men and women who depict today's standards of ideal physical appearance. They are the only type of people who seem to be having sex. They are also the ones who seem to need help in having *better* sex.

A rippled male stomach appears in a Tylenol ad. A beefy mountain climber is seen in a Ray•Ban sunglasses ad. An equally buffed man shows up in a Coppertone sunscreen ad. In an advertisement for Diesel clothing, a naked male flight attendant walks down the aisle of a plane while women grab, grope, and prod his sculpted body. An ad for fat-reducing tablets places a photograph of an incredibly sculpted man beside a photograph of Michelangelo's *David*. There is the beautiful and aching man in the Advil ad. There is the gorgeous man in an Edge shaving gel ad showing eight different kinds of gel for men's varying skin types.

Clinique's Turnaround Lotion "helps a man's skin look healthy and fit." Clinique also markets a facial scrub which claims that, "in just two minutes, this man's face is going to look terrific." There is Aramis's Lift Off! Moisture Formula, "created specifically to offer men fresher, younger-looking skin." There is Ralph Lauren's Face Fitness Moisture Formula that will "shape up [a man's] face in just two weeks."

IF IT SAYS SO IN A MAGAZINE, IT MUST BE TRUE

Although print advertisements reach millions of consumers in various periodicals and publications, they alone are not responsible for creating an ideal image of manhood and masculinity. Over the last several years more and more men's magazines have become available and have given men plenty of self-help articles. Men's magazines advertise male sexuality and an ideal male lifestyle through so-called life-enhancing articles and columns that play with, tease, and distort ideas of male self-esteem and self-confidence.

Health and appearance are the dominant topics covered by men's magazines. Whether the magazine is *Men's Health, Men's Fitness, Men's Journal,* or *Gentlemen's Quarterly,* the man on the cover is always the picture of perfect health and grooming. Inside the magazines, tucked in between the advertisements, are articles on such topics as the pros and cons of chest hair, penis size, better sex, and better love. These articles tell the same stories and promulgate the same propaganda as the advertisements.

An article in *Men's Health,* titled "Return of the Thin Man," gives readers advice on buying the right clothes to hide an overweight body. It seems there are men out there who simply cannot lose weight no matter how much they diet or exercise. The purpose of the article is to give hope to these men. If they can't change their bodies to fit within the standards of today's ideal men, here's how to hide that body and, at least, give the appearance of being ideal. "When it comes to choosing clothes," the article begins, "there's no point accentuating one's weaknesses." In other words, if you are fat, do everything you can to hide the fat because no one wants a fat man and his obvious faults.[11]

Men's magazines stress that for men to become what they are meant to be, they must exercise, exercise, exercise. *Gentlemen's Quarterly* makes its point immediately. The first sentence of an article in the magazine's "Personal Best" column reads, "Words you never want to hear from your girlfriend: small, spindly, limp." No, this isn't an article on penis enlargement; it is an article on how working out with dumbbells can give men the body they, and their girlfriends, want.[12]

"Hey, nobody said it was going to be pretty," begins a blurb in *Exercise for Men Only.* Accompanying the blurb is a photograph of a man lifting a dumbbell, his bicep bulging, his upper body smudged with grease, and his scowling face aimed directly at the camera. Not only is he handsome; he is mean—the kind of man men need to be to become "the best of everything."[13]

Exercise for Men Only also gives advice to male teens in an article titled "Weight Training for Teens, Building a Strong Foundation." The articles states that "strength of body will lead to more success on the sports field and a more muscular, trim physique will be more attractive to young women." Young males need to start young if they want to grow up to be real adult men. Only through extensive weight training will young men achieve the kind of body girls will notice.[14] What better preparation for adulthood than a strong body that will lead to both athletic and sexual success?

In the July 1994 issue of *Men's Workout,* there are several articles on exercise and weight-lifting routines. In between these are articles on workout injuries and their treatments, back problems, the importance of fluids in the body, penis size, and the danger of too much exposure to the sun. Each of these articles has, at its beginning, a photograph of a near-naked man, wearing only a pair of jeans or a tight-fitting pair of spandex shorts or other form-fitting workout wear. When an article is continued on a later page, another photograph of a near-naked man appears, stimulating the reader's interest enough to finish the article.

More of the same visuals can be found in the May 1994 issue of *Fitness Plus,* accompanying an article on nitrous oxide (laughing gas) and another on back injuries. Surely no plausible relationship exists between a well-built, hairless, white male body and laughing gas or back injuries. It is obvious that the editors of these magazines are using titillating photographs to attract certain readers and sub-scribers.

In leafing through some of the men's exercise magazines, it is easy for the mind to slip into thinking that you are looking instead through *Playgirl* or a gay male erotic magazine. The men used to illustrate various articles and exercise routines are obviously chosen very care-fully and for reasons that go beyond a beautiful face and body.

A careful examination of how men are posed in exercise magazine photographs and of what they are wearing (or, in some cases, what they are not wearing) leaves no question of a homoerotic message. The majority of the pages in exercise magazines for men are dedi-cated to showing and explaining various workout routines and regi-mens. Men are posed on or around exercise machines, or they are photographed holding certain types of free weights. The exercise machines or weights the models hold are props more than they are anything else. The models might just as well be standing among fallen Greek or Roman ruins and holding lyres or jugs of wine. What is most apparent in these photographs are the bodies and the clothing that accentuates certain body parts. Most notable are the genitals, the outlines of which are very clear.

Is there a legitimate reason for a photograph in an exercise magazine to show a sweaty man standing with nothing more than a towel hung between his legs? What exercise routine is explained with a photograph of a man wearing only skintight shorts, sitting on a bench with dumbbells resting on his knees, his legs spread apart in a way that immediately draws the reader's eyes to the bulge of his genitals? In the photograph below this one, the model has closed his legs, but the bulge of his genitals is visible still, and the weights are simply hanging to either side of the bench. It is difficult to comprehend the exercise benefits of letting weights that were once resting on your knees simply fall to the side of the workout bench.

Another photograph shows a man lying face down on a bench, angled in such a way that it pushes up his spandex-clad buttocks. The trainer stands over the reclining man with a hand resting on the small of the reclining man's back. The trainer stares into the camera, seemingly more interested in being photographed than with helping the other man properly use the exercise equipment. It is easy to interpret this photograph as a suggestion of impending anal intercourse—the roles of "top" and "bottom" clearly defined—than to interpret it as an illustration of how a trainer might make working out easier and more fulfilling.

Articles on cosmetic surgery for men frequently appear in men's exercise magazines and are just as frequently illustrated with photographs of well-sculpted men. One particular magazine goes a step further. Needless to say, the model is handsome and buffed; he is also sweaty and unsmiling. At the very bottom edge of the photograph is a clear view of an inch or so of his pubic hair. Gay male readers no doubt find this exciting or titillating. Are straight men comfortable with seeing male pubic hair in their exercise magazines? Either the publisher knows more about straight men than the rest of us, or he knows exactly the sexual preference of those who subscribe and buy this particular magazine and caters to them accordingly. Pubic hair is never shown in other men's exercise magazines, such as *Muscle & Fitness* or *Men's Fitness.*

Throughout sports history, bodybuilding has continuously maintained an overtone of homoeroticism. Bodybuilding magazines in past decades were widely purchased by gay men when no other form of gay-oriented erotic publications were available. The association became so common that *Muscle & Fitness* magazine, one of the most widely circulated men's exercise magazines, had to resort to using female models on the covers and inside pages of the magazine.

Whereas *Muscle & Fitness* makes an effort to dispel myths of homosexuality in the world of bodybuilding, the other fitness magazines do not.[15] The absence of women in several men's exercise magazines also helps to suggest an intended audience. In an issue of *Fitness Plus*, women appear only in five advertisements, three of which are sexual in nature. In the nearly 150-page, 1994 edition of *Exercise for Men Only*, women appear only in three ads, one of which is sexual in nature. An issue of *Men's Workout* includes eight ads featuring women, five of which are sexual in nature.

It has been said that exercise magazines, particularly those published by Joe Weider, publisher of *Muscle & Fitness*, "have two manifest functions: the sale of merchandise and the spread of ideology."[16] It is interesting that ideology is identified as a function of exercise magazines and not, for example, instruction. Clearly then, exercise magazines for men, Weider's as well as other publishers', are concerned with selling and promoting their respective doctrines on the appearance of the male body more than they are with giving actual bodybuilding or weight-training advice.

Espousing ideology is not limited to exercise magazines, however. The December 1994 issue of *Details* magazine uses a photo spread with a holiday office party as its theme to advertise various designer clothing for men and women. The models used in the photo spread, both male and female, are made to appear drunk. Liquor or beer shows up in almost every one of the seven full-page photographs. Most of the photographs are accompanied by clever captions to further the spirit of the party. "Keep your desk clean and don't abuse company equipment," is the caption used with a photograph showing a male party guest pinned down on a desk by a female party guest.

The following photograph shows the same man with his pants pulled down, standing in front of a copying machine while other party guests look on in hysterics.

The next photograph is shot from underneath a glass-top table. A man's face lays against the glass tabletop, suggesting he has passed out, or is about to, even though in his outstretched hands is a glass being filled with beer by another party guest.

The facing photograph shows a man lying on his back on the floor of the men's room, his body half in and half out of the stall. To the side of the downed man stands another man calmly drying his hands underneath the automatic hand dryer. The caption for these two photographs reads, "Get into the holiday spirits. But never lie down on the job."

In the photo spread's final photograph, a man and a woman are underneath another glass-top table. They both reach around to the tabletop and grab a glass full of white wine. The woman's other hand rests on the man's thigh. "Don't let the glass ceiling stop you from making advances," the copy reads.

The models used in this photo spread are all young and what can only be considered hip by today's standards. They obviously care about what kind of clothes they wear. This photo spread, however, is more than a fashion promotion. It is, by virtue of its captions, posings, and props, a promotion for alcohol abuse and sexual harassment. According to *Details* magazine, this is the lifestyle that should be desired and pursued by today's younger adults, if they want to be considered successful.

Men's magazines are not the only ones perpetuating male stereotypes. Women's magazines do as well. Men and male bodies appear less frequently in print advertisements found in women's magazines, but this does not mean that women's magazines are exempt from educating their readers on what does and does not constitute male beauty.

Along with their own promotion of the female beauty myth, women's magazines offer women an abundance of how-to or self-help articles on love, sex, and romance. At the beginning of these articles, there is typically a photograph of a naked or near-naked male/female couple, meant to visually represent both the subject of the article and the all-American heterosexual relationship. Naturally, because the photographs appear in women's magazines, the female models are thin, white, and beautiful. Naturally, again because they are women's magazines educating women on what their mates must look like, the male models are well-defined, white, usually without body hair, and attractive.

As women and men leaf through their respective magazines, they see and begin to comprehend the new male sex symbol who is epitomized by his whiteness, muscularity, handsomeness, lack of body hair, and penis, more than likely, above-average in size. This is how men appear whether they are centerfolds in *Playgirl,* models in *Gentlemen's Quarterly,* the average lover exemplified in *Cosmopolitan* and *Glamour,* or simply the everyday men in *Men's Fitness.* Their images are frozen in photographs. Their worth is characterized by silent immovable bodies meant only to titillate, to enthrall, and to promote an ideal as an accepted norm.

HERE'S THE BEEF

Similar to print advertising and visual illustrations of self-help, how-to, and lifestyle-enhancing articles, television commercials have come a long way in how they depict men and male bodies. Over the last several years more and more naked men have been popping up in television commercials, selling everything from cars to deodorants to shaving products to clothing to beverages. As different as the products are in what they do or provide, the male bodies used to sell them are, for the most part, the same.

A car commercial tells us that the design of the car's body was inspired by the human body—"sleek and curvy." Flashes of well-built, near-naked male bodies blink across the television screen, superimposed with the car. Cars, or at least this particular car, are no longer a simple means of transportation that gets us from one place to another. Cars must be sleek, curvy, powerful, dependable, and long lasting. When we see, over and over again, a commercial comparing a car's body to a human body, we cannot expect our bodies and the bodies of our spouses and partners to be anything less than sleek, curvy, strong, powerful, dependable, and long lasting. After all, "[d]oesn't everyone want a little more muscle?" asks another car commercial. Chevrolet trucks are strong "like a rock," and the makers of Lexus automobiles brag about their "relentless pursuit of perfection." Only the strong and the perfect need purchase these vehicles. Only they are worthy of owning them and of being behind the wheel.

Shaving products for men also are advertised with great frequency in television commercials, and most of these commercials feature ample quantities of near-naked male bodies. "Hey, Remington. Shave this," taunts a handsome man with visible hair growth on his face. "The best a man can get" is what Gillette will have us believe about their razors and shaving products and the men who use them.

One of the most blatant television commercials for shaving products that stereotypes men and male good looks is a commercial for Braun shavers. At the beginning of the commercial, a man and a woman are buying a magazine before boarding a train. They carry identical briefcases, and both set them on the floor while they look through the magazine rack. The woman leaves first. She bends down and by mistake picks up the briefcase belonging to the man. Once on board the train, she opens the briefcase and discovers a Braun electric razor. Clearly she has the wrong briefcase. She leaves her seat and goes in search of the man who might have her briefcase. As she walks through the train she looks at various male passengers, casually but sternly rejecting several men as the possible owner of the briefcase, solely on their physical appearance. She passes by an ordinary-looking ticket taker. For a split second, she notices a man of color who is wearing glasses, only to pass him by. She glances at a man who has a beard and a receding hairline whom she rejects. The woman stops only when she spots the attractive, clean-shaven, white man sitting alone.

While the commercial is running, the narrator says, "[T]he most revealing thing about the man who uses a Braun is how easy it is to spot him." Men who use Braun shavers are men who "appreciate good looks," although it is unclear whether these men appreciate their own good looks or the good looks of women. Even though there are plenty of other men on the train, only the man who is considered attractive has "the world's most recognized shave" because he has the world's most recognized and desired face. He is the type of man women want and the type of man most men want to be.

One of the most surprising uses of the male body in a television commercial is an advertisement for Celestial Seasonings tea. The narration for this commercial uses phrases such as "herbal tea with real body," "exotic combinations," "powerfully delicious," and "perfectly balanced." All of these phrases seem to be appropriate descriptions of herbal teas. Even the twice-repeated phrase, "the way tea ought to be," is a fair and just way of ranking this particular brand of tea over any other brand. However, what happens when, during the narration, we are shown, from several different camera angles, a well-built, handsome, white man wearing only a pair of skintight shorts? Suddenly, "the way tea ought to be" becomes the way men's bodies ought to be—exotic, powerfully delicious, and perfectly balanced. Tea "with real body" becomes men with real bodies.

Television commercials share with print advertisements the ability to promote standards of ideal male beauty. In addition, television commercials share with print advertisements the ability to promote stereotypes of masculinity, male thinking, and male behavior. If a men's movement has given birth to new men, these new men have not completely taken over the realm of television advertising. Old stereotypes of who men are and what they do remain fixed in modern-day television commercials.

Consider a commercial for Haggar clothing that says, "Where is it written that men should always get the backbreaking, sweaty jobs? Is it stamped into a man's genetic code that he would rather paint houses, fix carburetors, move furniture? Maybe a guy would rather just stay at home and iron pants. Yeah, right." There is a possibility that men can move away from old stereotypes, but in the end, they do not seem to want to—not if it means staying at home and ironing pants.

Another commercial for Haggar even pokes fun at new male stereotypes: "I'm just a guy. And I don't have to think about what I wear because I've got a lot of important guy things to do." At the end of this commercial, the man is seen going into the bathroom carrying a newspaper. This is the important "guy thing" this man has to do.

Other commercials exploiting past notions of masculinity and manhood are commercials for the military. "Be all you can be," invites the United States Army, with television ads that offer men the chance to play with tanks and missiles. The United States Marines glorifies killing and defines manhood with life-sized chess pieces destroying one another: "To compete you've got to be strong. To win you've got to be smart. Maybe you can be one of us. The few, the proud, the Marines."

Military commercials go beneath muscles and grab men where it really hurts—their pride and their allegiance to the United States: "[Men] should be able to kill or be killed in defense of [their] famil[ies], [their] country, or even [their] manhood." Is this what military commercials are telling men about manhood? Women are in the military. Are they being told that killing in defense of family and country is a condition of their womanhood? It seems unlikely when we "[c]onsider what would have to be done to women's hearts and minds for them to accept the role of killing other women or being killed by other women as proof of their womanhood." We live in a society that cannot imagine the possibility of women killing women. The same society, however, has no trouble imagining men killing men and condones such killing in its military advertising.[17]

We have seen what advertising is doing to and with men and their bodies. How, then, is this affecting the self-esteem of men in the real world? Does advertising play a key role in creating personalities and shaping our ideals of what is and is not attractive in men?

Images of women in advertising that create stereotypes of femininity and female beauty have long been recognized as being damaging to women. Women in ads become role models for everyday women, and these everyday women do whatever it takes to live up to the standards that advertising images create. Are similar role models being created for men?

In her book, *The Beauty Myth,* Naomi Wolf writes that "[m]en are exposed to male *fashion* models but do not see them as *role* models."[18] This might have been true in the past, when images of men were more limited, when being male—any kind of male—would do. The original Marlboro Man, for example, was accepted as an image of manliness mainly because of his cowboy gear and his horse. No one really cared about what the Marlboro Man looked like; his persona was enough. The original Marlboro Man was more an idea than an ideal.

A great majority of advertising aimed at women, either in print or on television, concerns appearance. What is created in these ads are role models for women. As we have seen in the advertisements described previously, a great deal of advertising aimed at men, in print or on television, is about men looking better or about feeling better by first looking better. The Marlboro Man is no longer an idea; he is an *ideal* because in current Marlboro ads the Marlboro Man is younger, more attractive, less wrinkled, and no doubt has a muscular body underneath his cowboy gear. The Marlboro Man and all the other men in current-day advertisements aimed at men have become *role* models. The emphasis is not on cowboy clothes and horses as superficial representations of masculinity: the emphasis is on faces and bodies.

Facial and body attractiveness are but two components meant to define manhood and masculinity. Because "[m]asculinity is judged by overall appearance and impression," a handsome face and a muscular body are not enough, despite what is espoused by many advertisements. Ads instruct men further: "The commercials on television will suggest the main attributes a man needs to be considered attractive and desirable."[19]

The advertising industry complicates being a man in today's world, making it very clear that to be a man one must "take it like a man." Masculinity is billed as strength, and "men by and large still want products that are 'tough,' even to the point of pain—aftershave stings because men like that."[20] Discounting or rejecting certain masochistic behaviors, is there any man who wants to feel or enjoys feeling pain? Are we to believe that men truly enjoy the sting of aftershave? The advertising industry, or at least those who write about the industry, seems to want us to believe that men do—that men inherently know that to be or feel masculine they must be able to handle certain pain, even enjoy it. This places a heavy burden upon men. It is difficult enough for most men to live up to stereotyped and overblown physical images of masculinity and manhood. Adding to these the psychological stereotypes of pain acceptance and expectation is more than unfair; it is cruel. It is hardly coincidental, then, that military commercials air so frequently during football games and other sports broadcasts. The aim is to be men, to feel pain, and to win, no matter what the cost.

The cost of stereotyping men in advertising, whether they are stereotyped as beautiful hunks or aggressive killers, is the undermining of men's self-esteem through sexism, or rather reverse sexism. To survive, the advertising industry now picks on men because it can no longer get away with picking on women. Feminists and women's organizations have lobbied to change the way women are depicted in advertising, though plenty of ads and commercials still exist that are sexist toward women. The majority of advertisements and commercials for household cleaning products, for example, continue to use and target women. Main characters in ads and commercials for cold remedy products are mostly women, mothers in particular—"Dr. Mom," says one television commercial for a cough syrup. Despite the strides made on behalf of equality, in the eyes of the advertising industry, women are still predominately homemakers and caretakers and not much more.

The use of men as sex objects in ads is nothing more than a clever attempt by the advertising industry to cover up its continued portrayal of women as the weaker sex. Since most of the attention placed on these ads focuses on reverse sexism—men as sex objects—the sexism against women almost disappears—almost, but not quite.

The most glaring example of this is the famous and infamous Diet Coke commercial in which women are shown staring at a hunky construction worker as he strips off his shirt. At first glance, this commercial epitomizes reverse sexism. Instead of men ogling feminine beauty, women ogle masculine beauty. Turnabout is fair play, or so it seems. A closer look at this commercial reveals more than reverse sexism.

Although the Diet Coke commercial does introduce new stereotypes of men and women, exploiting modern ideals of masculinity and femininity, it also perpetuates old stereotypes. Men are construction workers, while the women are "a bunch of office workers," presumably secretaries or members of a corporate typing pool, given the look and feel of their office environment.[21] Reverse sexism—the man as the sex object—in the Diet Coke commercial is superficial, yet it succeeds in effectively disguising the true essence of the commercial's message: roles for men and women haven't changed much at all.

The Diet Coke commercial made this male model a celebrity. His face and body made him a star. He has his own calendar and workout video. He made his prime-time acting debut on NBC's *Wings*, in which one of the show's female characters rips his shirt off to expose his famous chest. When was the last time we saw, on prime-time television, a man rip off a woman's blouse and expose her breasts to millions of viewers? Such a thing would be considered an act of aggression, perhaps even rape, if it were done to a woman by a man. When done to a man by a woman, however, the act of aggression is portrayed as erotic and exciting, even funny. The idea or suggestion of rape is never considered, although this is exactly what it is when a woman rips off the shirt from a man's body simply for the sake of seeing his chest. The seriousness of the act is not lessened by the fact that it occurs in a televised situation comedy. There is nothing humorous about nonconsensual sexual aggression directed at men.

Yet humor is a main ingredient in commercials that reverse the normally accepted roles of men and women. A perfect example of this is a television commercial for the Hyundai Elantra. Two women stand at the top of a short staircase and watch as various cars pull into a parking lot. Most of the cars are expensive sports car models, and they are all driven by men. As the men get out of their cars, the two women comment on what "shortcomings" these men must be making up for by driving expensive sports cars. When up pulls the sensibly priced Hyundai Elantra driven by a handsome white man, one of the women says to the other, "I wonder what he's got under his hood?" The ad copy across the screen reads, "Solid, well-built and long-lasting. Actually, we're talking about the car." Actually, they're not talking about the car; they're talking about the man just as the women are. This commercial touches upon almost every standard stereotype applied to men, both old and new. The man in the commercial is smart enough to buy a sensibly priced car, he is handsome and no doubt has a well-built body underneath his carefully chosen clothes, and the size of his penis is important to the women who watch him and most likely to himself as well.

Within a month after this commercial began to air, Elantra sales increased by 8 percent. In the following month, sales increased by 50 percent.[22] Obviously then, using men as sex symbols and objects of sexism does work when it comes to successfully selling a product. Jerry Wilson, the founder of Soloflex, makes this point very clear. In 1985, Soloflex began using advertisements with hard-bodied celebrities such as Ken Norton, Frank Zane, and Mitch Gaylord. "A hard man is good to find," reads the ad copy. Sales of Soloflex exercise machines increased by 20 percent after the ad started to run.[23]

Why is the Elantra commercial funny? It wouldn't be if the roles were reversed. If two men spent a few minutes commenting on the cars driven by women and on the size of their breasts, many would be in an uproar because of the overt sexism. Where is the outrage about the overt sexism toward men? Apparently there isn't any. "[R]ole-reversed ogling, with men as objects and women doing the gawking, doesn't push the same buttons." In the end, it is dismissed as being cute.[24] It is also a blatant double standard that should not be allowed. Men are criticized and verbally castrated when they behave as male chauvinist pigs, but women are allowed and encouraged to be female chauvinist pigs. Is this what women want when they scream for equality? Is this what men want? The truth of this is that no one is being made equal to anyone else. Women are not becoming the equals of men simply because society, or at least the advertising industry, allows them to treat men as they themselves have been treated. Reverse sexism is no better than sexism. Commercials, such as the ones for Diet Coke and Hyundai, simply ". . . perpetuate the same patriarchal, sexist thinking," says Diane Welsh of the New York chapter of the National Organization for Women.[25] Media critic and documentary filmmaker Jean Kilbourne agrees, saying that while role reversals may be instructive this instruction does not make things equal between men and women.[26]

No wonder men are confused about how they should behave and about what is the definition *du jour* of masculinity. On the one hand, men are being told they should break away from past stereotypes of masculinity and embrace the stereotypes of new men. Some members of society want today's men to care more about their appearance and about what clothes and cologne they wear. On the other hand, men are being told that the old stereotypes are just fine, that it is okay to be auto mechanics and bathroom readers. They are manly and masculine because they can paint houses, fix carburetors, move furniture, and sit on the toilet and read the sports page for as long as they like.

*　　*　　*

Is it possible that men might begin to fear sexual and emotional rejection by women because they do not live up to male standards in advertising? Since unattractive and overweight men are seen less often in advertising than their polar opposites, it is more than feasible that women in the real world will begin to ignore or discount these men as desired emotional or sexual mates. This possible scenario is brought to life in a chewing gum commercial in which an overweight man sucks in his stomach as he passes by two slim, bikini-clad, beautiful women. Because of the size of his stomach, he knows he doesn't stand a chance with these women. By sucking in his gut, he speaks for men everywhere. He has no fear of physical violence from these women, but because he cannot be seen in public the way he truly is—a man with a large stomach—he manifests emotional violence against himself. He is doomed to a life alone. This commercial, along with a myriad of others like it, sends a very clear message to men: if you want women, be beautiful and muscular men; otherwise, women will not take notice.

The idea is to "keep America beautiful," as a clean-faced teenage boy says in a Clearasil commercial. But at what cost? Naomi Wolf theorizes that a male beauty myth could be more damaging to men than the female counterpart was to women. More men are expected to begin to suffer from eating disorders. Contemporary projections of an idealized male body are telling men what women want, in the same way the projection of an idealized female body has told women what men want. Wolf concludes that, if this is the case, everyone loses.[27]

Advertising tells us that the Western world ought to be populated with beautiful people only. We are led to believe that advertisements and commercials are pictures of real people doing, wearing, saying, and showing real things, a belief that is equally the perception made by the viewer and the intent created by the advertiser. "[I]t hardly needs stressing [that] men and women take their cues about 'gender behavior' from the image of that behavior that advertising throws back at them, and they contrive to become the 'people' in those ads."[28] An accepted component of current-day gender behavior is that men and women cannot tolerate someone who isn't beautiful. The man who has a fifty-inch waist and the pimply-faced teenage boy are ignored and forgotten. They are not real because we do not see them in advertisements and television commercials.

When looking at advertisements and television commercials, it is important to remember that all of what we are viewing is intended to be there.[29] The type of men used in advertisements and commercials are chosen carefully. What the men look like has little to do with the product they are selling but a great deal to do with the image and lifestyle being sold. The men and male bodies seen in ads and commercials for cars, grooming products, exercise equipment, better-sex videos, clothing, and cologne are very different from the men and male bodies seen in ads and commercials for, for example, diarrhea medicines, cough syrups, and insurance. Advertisements would have us believe that only beautiful men use Gillette shaving and grooming products and only beautiful men wear Jockey underwear and Jordache or Levi's jeans. Advertisements would have us believe that unattractive men do not shave, or if they do, they do not care what shaving does to their skin and ultimately to their overall look. Advertising would have us believe that beautiful men never get diarrhea or colds.

Advertising has enormous power. The images and messages delivered from ads can and do alter the way we think and how we feel about other people. More important, ads have tremendous influence on the way we think and how we feel about ourselves. If men buy what the ads are selling, they pay for it with deeply eroded self-esteem and shattered self-confidence. Perhaps, however, self-esteem and self-confidence do not matter in a society that values outside appearance—how we look to other people—more than anything else. As a General Nutrition Center ad for a vitamin supplement asks, "Why be an ordinary man when you can be a Mega Man?"

Chapter 5

Me Tarzan, You Wimp: Films

According to the *Movie Buff Checklist: A History of Male Nudity in the Movies*, it was John Huston's *The Bible . . . In the Beginning* (1966) that gave moviegoers their first real taste of the naked male body in film.[1] At the start of this film, the blond-haired Adam (Michael Parks) is seen lying on the ground in all of his naked glory. Was it merely a coincidence that Michael Parks was handsome, trim, and muscular, or are we to believe that somewhere in the cosmos from which he came there was a gym and God was Adam's personal trainer?

By 1971, the number of scenes in Hollywood movies featuring male nudity reached its highest, cresting at 100.[2] This comes as no surprise, given the tenor of the 1970s, a decade in which one of the hottest fads was streaking. A public display of male flesh seemed almost commonplace in the 1970s, on and off the movie screen.

In looking back at exposed male bodies in films from the silent movie era through the late 1970s, one question that arises is this: Did audiences care about what these male bodies looked like or were they simply attracted to the raw and daring public display of suggested sex? The nude or near-nude male body, regardless of what it looked like physically, may have been enough for audiences of the 1970s and earlier. The presence of the body was all that mattered. However, the culture of the 1970s was not like the cultures of the 1980s or 1990s. Male body worship had not yet become so widely popular. Although the male actors of the 1970s and earlier did have certain similarities in the way their bodies appeared, their bodies were noticed and appreciated in much different ways than the bodies of male actors appearing in films of the 1980s and 1990s. Remarking on male nudity in a movie, an audience member of the 1960s or

1970s might have asked, "Can you believe he was naked?" Remarking similarly on male nudity in a film from the 1980s or early 1990s, an audience member is more likely to have asked, "Can you believe how great his body looked?"

GOOD BODIES

Beginning in the early 1980s, there was a drastic change in the physical appearance of men in film. Violence became a required ingredient if a film was to become a blockbuster. Who better to instigate or oppose violence than a hero, a fighter of evil, so that good may prevail?

The 1980s was the decade of the hero-driven movie. The necessary bodily quality a movie hero must possess to combat the evil he encounters is muscles. Consequently, it became imperative for actors in movies of the 1980s and early 1990s to have well-built, often extreme physiques. The most obvious of these actors are Arnold Schwarzenegger, Sylvester Stallone, and Jean-Claude Van Damme. These three actors epitomize male perfection and, some will argue, masculinity in the films of the 1980s and early 1990s.[3] To a lesser muscular extent, but certainly not to a lesser beauty extent, so too did Bruce Willis, Mel Gibson, Kevin Costner, and Tom Cruise. It is relevant to note that the bodies of Willis, Gibson, Costner, and Cruise are still considered attractive and well-defined enough to have the actors frequently appear in nude scenes. In other words, they are still physically attractive enough to establish an ideal. What Willis, Gibson, Costner, and Cruise lack in muscularity is made up for in facial attractiveness and overall sex appeal to female and gay male movie viewers.

The actors who dominated movies in the 1980s and early 1990s became enormously visible symbols of maleness and masculinity. Their celebrity status made them role models for millions of men and young boys. What pre- or postpubescent male wouldn't want to grow up to look like Schwarzenegger, Stallone, or Van Damme? What full-grown man wouldn't want to look like these actors? They always win, and they always get the girl.

The characters these actors play, and subsequently the actors themselves, all have the kind of body that in the end represents the ideal body. It is their bodies that have made them stars, not their ability to act. Their "heroic bodies" made the films they appeared in blockbusters, collectively raking in hundreds of millions of dollars for the studios.[4]

A movie is successful if it makes a lot of money. Artistic value is generally secondary to bottom-line profits. Likewise, an actor's acting ability is often secondary to his physical appearance. In the eyes of the Hollywood studios, Schwarzenegger, Stallone, and Van Damme are more valuable than, for example, Woody Allen, Danny DeVito, or Steve Martin. This is not to say that Allen, DeVito, Martin, and other actors who have a following do not make money for Hollywood studios. They do. However, none of their films can rightfully be called a blockbuster. It is unlikely that many men or boys want to look like them. It is equally unlikely that many women or gay men want to see them naked.

In the 1950s, moviegoers wanted to see a Rock Hudson film because the film starred Rock Hudson. Although it is true that Hudson, during his reign as a matinee idol, was a symbol of the ultimate American he-man (his homosexuality notwithstanding), his symbol of such was not dependent on how his body looked. Moviegoers in the 1950s and 1960s never had the chance to see Hudson's naked or near-naked body. Hudson didn't appear fully naked in a film until 1976 (*Embryo*), and because of clever lighting, not much of his body could be seen.[5] Hudson kept his clothes on and still managed to maintain his position as he-man.

Flesh is money in the movies, as much as it is in advertising and literature. Hollywood knows as well as Madison Avenue that sex sells. A large part of what made movies so successful in the 1980s and early 1990s were the muscular male bodies—white male bodies—coupled with a requisite amount of violence. Violence can sell on its own, but if the characters on screen instigating the violence are not pleasant to look at, movie audiences may feel cheated or short-changed.

Movie audiences expect to see the "hard bodies" that made movies in the 1980s and 1990s so successful. As Susan Jeffords explains, male "soft bodies" of the 1970s were the norm in movies made in that decade, and these "soft body" movies reflected the "soft body" masculinity that prevailed in 1970s society. It was the early 1980s when the norm shifted.[6]

Upon seeing Stallone in *First Blood* (1982), movie audiences in the early 1980s, according to Jeffords, were seeing something they hadn't seen before—the pumped-up male body exemplified by Rambo/Stallone. Audiences liked what they were seeing, so they wanted more. Jeffords considers this the reason for *First Blood*'s success.[7] As Antony Easthope remarks in *What a Man's Gotta Do*, "Images of the hard, trained, disciplined body under rational control are not just there to be identified with—they are there to be looked at."[8] This is the difference between, for example, the bodies of Hudson and Cruise—Hudson's body is to be identified with, while Cruise's body is to be looked at. Likewise, Stallone's, Schwarzenegger's, and Van Damme's bodies are to be looked at as well. More than being seen, the bodies of these actors are to be envied and desired—envied because male audiences want to look like these actors and desired because female and gay male audiences want to be with these actors or, rather, the bodies of these actors.

Following the success of *First Blood* and the success of Stallone's body, the muscular male body remained a movie and lifestyle marketing tool throughout the 1980s and into the 1990s. Other Ramboesque bodies and movies were released, raking in huge amounts of money for the studios and making stars out of the hard-bodied actors. Well-developed pectoral muscles and defined abdominal muscles became mandatory requirements of male actors. Their bodies were nothing less than perfect. Their ability to act, on the other hand, was often criticized. As one writer remarked on the actor Van Damme, "[he] has long been expected to act only with his pecs and his abs."[9] The same can be said for a number of male actors who appeared in the blockbuster films of the 1980s and 1990s. These pecs and abs, made larger than life on movie screens all over the world, made it abundantly clear that the good guys must always have equally good bodies.

BAD BODIES

In the movies, we also have the bad guys, and, more often than not, the bad guys are less attractive and less well-built than the good guys, continuing the notion that bad equals ugly. As the good guys—the heroes—Stallone, Schwarzenegger, Van Damme, and the rest are, for the most part, bigger and better looking than their on-screen adversaries. This was necessary for the audience to believe and accept these characters as heroes. In all the Rambo films, in *The Terminator* and *Terminator 2: Judgement Day,* and in films such as *Robocop, Batman, Batman Returns, Lethal Weapon, Die Hard,* and *Die Hard 2: Die Harder,* "the heroic body turns out to be like Rambo's, superior to those of his enemies, his companions, *and* the audience."[10] What is most relevant here is the hero's body being superior to the body of any given male member of a movie audience. No man wants to be seen as a bad guy, and no man wants to look like a bad guy is supposed to look—soft-bodied. In this context, Hollywood's message to male movie viewers is a simple one: be good and strong; be a hero, not a bad guy.

What happens, though, when one of the bad guys is also a hard body? What happens when Hollywood gives us a character such as Carl in *Ghost*?

Carl (Tony Goldwyn) throws a curve into the notion that only the good guys in movies have the good or hard bodies. In the scene in which Carl purposely spills coffee on himself, only to create an excuse to take off his shirt, the audience is treated to a set of well-developed, highly prized, and highly desired pectoral and abdominal muscles. Carl attempts to seduce Molly (Demi Moore) both by playing on Molly's vulnerability and loneliness, resulting from the sudden death of her husband (played by hard-bodied actor Patrick Swayze), and with his desirable body. This scene in the film could only work with an actor who has a body such as Goldwyn's. Even before Carl spills the coffee, it is clear that his intention is to entice Molly into having sex with him. If Carl were to not take his shirt off, and not reveal the attractive, sexy body underneath, he would simply remain the film's bad guy. The moment his shirt comes off, he becomes something different. Because of his physical beauty/perfection, he is a *sexy* bad guy. The audience's attention is drawn toward his good body, focusing on him sexually and ready to overlook, if just for a moment, his hideous behavior.

Molly almost gives in, nearly surrenders to Carl's physical beauty/perfection. In the end, however, she is too distraught over the death of her equally attractive husband to go through with it. Maybe later, after she has had enough time to grieve for her dead husband, she can return to this beautiful man and give in to her and to his desires. After all, at this point in the film, Molly does not know that Carl was responsible for her husband's death.

What stands out most in this scene from *Ghost* is Carl's knowing exactly what he must do, what he must *show* to win Molly's affections. His body is his strongest weapon. He is not bad enough to kill with a real weapon—he hires someone to kill for him, someone who is not hard-bodied and would not be considered attractive. In other words, a real bad guy. Carl is not out to kill Molly. He is, however, out to get her, or more accurately, to have her sexually. He knows, because he is a "new" man, that what women desire in men is a good and healthy body. For what other reason would he accidentally spill coffee on himself? For what other reason would he expose his desirable body? His attempt to seduce Molly begins with and depends entirely upon the presentation of his chest and stomach, as if, in his mind and in Molly's mind, nothing else matters, not even the death of his friend, her husband.

Even Carl's brutal death at the end of the film is rendered moot or unimportant. His death heightens the film's drama and serves as ample conclusion to the story. More than a few people, however, who have seen or will see *Ghost* probably will remember the film more for its beautiful and hard-bodied stars than for its attempt to allegorize life and death or right and wrong. Carl is corrupted beauty, an alluring mix consisting of a beautiful body and a dangerous mind. He is dead by the film's end, but his body remains very much alive in the memories of moviegoers.

Another of the few examples of the hard-bodied bad guy in movies is the character Gaston in Disney's version of *Beauty and the Beast*. Disney is famous for turning old tales, fairy tales, into blockbuster movies. In *Beauty and the Beast,* Disney changes several points of the original story, no doubt in an attempt to make the film more appealing to a wider audience.

It is worth noting here Susan Jeffords' observation on how Disney's altering of the story relates to the subject of men in movies.[11] Jeffords notes (and research for this book concurs) that in other versions or translations of the story the cause of the curse and the curse itself are not explained until the end.[12] In fact, in some of the stories the Beast is not permitted to explain to Beauty, or to anyone, what the curse entails until it has been lifted. This is not the case in the Disney version, in which the reason for the curse is explained early in the film—a change that greatly alters the movie's meaning and impact.[13]

The Disney story ends up being the Beast's story, not Beauty's.[14] Ostensibly, it becomes a film about a *man's* search for love, but in reality, it is a film about a beast who is looking for love so he can be turned back into a young, handsome, rich prince. In the Disney film, the character of Beauty, for all intents and purposes, is merely a springboard for the Beast's return to real manhood.

Although it is true that at the end of the Disney film the Beast does love Beauty, and Beauty certainly loves the Beast, it is the restoration of the Beast's beautiful human form that becomes the central message of the film. In fairness to Disney, this same message is delivered in all of the other written versions of the story. The character we have come to love and respect during the course of the book or movie is replaced by a handsome and well-built stranger.

Gaston's physical appearance, even in animation, is important, containing all the elements so popular in movies.[15] So hard is Gaston's body, so much is his look that of the hypermasculine male, there seems to be a touch of Tom of Finland in the way Gaston has been drawn. His entire appearance, from head to toe, is pure exaggeration, pure fantasy. He is a modern-day bodybuilder, not unlike Rambo, plunked in the midst of a quaint storybook village.

Everything about Gaston is a stereotype—his carousing with the boys, his skill as a hunter, his inflated self-image as a lady-killer. As we listen to him speak, throughout the film, we realize that he epitomizes the phrase "God's gift to women." As Jeffords describes, Gaston spends his time terrorizing anyone ". . . who [does] not succumb to his good looks."[16]

The character of Gaston in *Beauty and the Beast* is similar to the character of Carl in *Ghost*, a bad guy with a good body. Their badness, though, is motivated by different reasons. Carl is bad because he arranges for a friend to be killed so he, Carl, can gain access to computer records from which he plans to steal several million dollars. Gaston, on the other hand, is motivated by conceit and by desire, but his desire is not for Beauty as much as it is his own desire for Beauty to love him and see him for what he is—a real man.

Gaston is willing to kill, and, like Rambo or the Terminator, has the muscles and weapons to accomplish his goal of killing the Beast. However, he kills, or is willing to kill, only because he wants to save the girl. He sets out to do what the fairy-tale hero is meant to do— save the damsel in distress. To be the hero, both for Beauty and for the audience, explains Gaston's existence in Disney's version of the story.

What is another reason for the addition of Gaston in the Disney version? The answer is simple. Without Gaston, the audience is given no male to identify with and no male body to desire. No one wants to identify with the Beast because he is a beast and his actions are beastly. No one wants to desire the Beast's body because it is ugly and hairy. Further, as was noted earlier, Disney's version of *Beauty and the Beast* is the Beast's story, not Beauty's. But the Beast is no hero. Gaston is the hero. Gaston is the one the audience is intended to identify with, and his body is the body the audience is supposed to desire, despite Gaston's beastly behavior, exhibited by his conceit and self-inflated ego. Without Gaston, Disney's *Beauty and the Beast* is simply another animated fairy tale brought to the big screen. Gaston saves the audience from having to wait until the film's end to find a character with whom they can identify—the ugly Beast turned into the handsome Prince.

This is the identical saving feature found in *Ghost*. Carl's body in *Ghost* plays the same role that Gaston's body plays in *Beauty and the Beast*. Carl's character is important to the story being told in *Ghost*, but it is his body that becomes the focal point of his presence in the film. Once Sam is killed and becomes a ghost, with no reason to take off his clothes, there is no male body to display or to be the object of desire.

SOFT BODIES, AGING SEX SYMBOLS, AND RUBBER SUITS

It has been suggested that Hollywood movies are beginning to change in the ways they represent masculinity and maleness. Some validity to this observation can be found when we look at some of the films that followed the Rambo and Terminator films. Jeffords names films such as *Field of Dreams, Robin Hood, The Doctor, Regarding Henry,* and *Switch* as examples of Hollywood products that internalize masculinity. These films use love and emotion to define masculinity, as opposed to machinery and weapons. "What Hollywood culture is offering, in place of the bold spectacle of male muscularity and/as violence," writes Jeffords, "is a self-effacing man, one who now, instead of learning to fight, learns to love."[17] Jeffords' point also can be directed toward other films, such as *Dances with Wolves, Interview with the Vampire, The Age of Innocence, Philadelphia,* and *Legends of the Fall.*

In these films, the display of the male body as an object of desire is less blatant, though the display, at least in some of these films, is still there. The lead male characters do spend the course of the movie learning more to love than to fight. Seemingly, the result of this "shifting focus" from externalized masculinity to internalized masculinity is the shifting focus from men's outer bodies to men's inner qualities.[18] To some extent, this is true. The bodies of the actors in these movies are different from the bodies in movies such as *First Blood, Die Hard,* and *The Terminator.* The bodies of Kevin Costner, Daniel Day-Lewis, or Tom Hanks are not like the bodies of Sylvester Stallone, Bruce Willis, or Arnold Schwarzenegger. Costner, Day-Lewis, and Hanks are less muscular, and the roles they play in their movies are less muscular. They are not meant to be action/adventure heroes; they are meant to be emotional heroes.

To be an emotional hero in the movies, an actor doesn't need the hypermasculine look required of the action/adventure hero. At the same time, however, his body, including his physique and facial appearance, still must fit within an accepted stereotype of male physical attractiveness. An element of male beauty still must be present. The bodies of actors such as Costner, Day-Lewis, and Hanks are certainly less muscular, but they are in no way physically unattractive or physically out of shape. Costner's body, for example, has none of the muscularity of Stallone's or Schwarzenegger's, but still, we see his naked body in several of his films. His body, although not muscular, is at least thin, a good enough reason to show him naked on screen.

Although the implication here may seem to suggest that Hollywood producers and filmmakers are *only* concerned with muscles and handsome faces, this is not altogether true. In some cases, certain male actors are cast more for their reputations as competent actors or successful draws than for the muscularity of their bodies or for their overall sex appeal. Hollywood does allow room for certain male actors who are not the physical equals of the likes of Schwarzenegger, Stallone, or Van Damme. Four examples of these less-appealing, yet popular, actors are Liam Neeson, Keanu Reeves, Jeremy Irons, and Daniel Day-Lewis. Each of these actors has played in successful films. For the most part, until recently, these actors have done this without taking off their clothes in the films in which they appeared.

Despite their success in nudity-free movies and their reputations of being popular actors, Neeson, Reeves, Irons, and Day-Lewis all have managed to find themselves cast in films in which an exhibition of flesh was required; Neeson in *Rob Roy,* Reeves in *Johnny Mnemonic,* Irons in *Die Hard with a Vengeance,* and Day-Lewis in *Last of the Mohicans.* In each of these films, and for the actors to more successfully play their respective male characters, their bodies had to change. This was crucial to the producers and to the filmmakers, and perhaps to the success of the film at the box office, because the stories and/or situations required an exposition of flesh. To satisfy this imperative element of the films, Neeson, Reeves, Irons, and Day-Lewis had to build up their bodies. This is obvious when you compare their bodies in earlier films to the appearance of their bodies in later films. Suddenly, the reputations of these actors was secondary to what they looked like with no or little clothing. Whatever sex appeal these four actors had before was replaced and enhanced by a sex appeal that became strongly dependent upon the appearance of their bodies.

Two other films relevant to any discussion on men, the male body, and masculinity are *Batman Forever* and *The Bridges of Madison County.* In both of these films, stereotyped male bodies and ideals of muscularity are apparent, either in their presence or in their absence.

In the first three Batman films, *Batman, Batman Returns,* and *Batman Forever,* the actor cast as Batman falls within the category of the typical Hollywood male sex symbol. The role of Batman in the first two films was a definite switch for actor Michael Keaton. Prior to *Batman*, Keaton was already a star and no doubt considered by some to be a Hollywood sex symbol. His sex symbol status, however, was more a result of his facial attractiveness or his charm or his sometimes blundering sensitivity.

As the alter ego of Bruce Wayne, Batman has to rely on aspects other than facial attractiveness, charm, and sensitivity. Batman is, after all, a fighter of evil, an action/adventure hero. We know from other Hollywood films that an action/adventure hero must have a very particular type of body. However, Keaton, at least while playing Batman, does not have to be concerned with the appearance of his body. His body is not important because the strength and musculature of Batman comes from a rubber suit. In this instance, it is the rubber suit that becomes the object of display and not the actual body of the actor. This does not mean, however, that a stereotype is not still perpetuated.

Batman's rubber suit is without question a manufactured replica of the hyped and stereotyped ideal male body. It has well-formed pectoral muscles and sculpted abdominal muscles, and includes an ample display of the genital area—a body befitting a hero. As Hollywood so blatantly exemplifies, no man can be a hero without big pectoral muscles, a sculpted or at least flat stomach, and, if not the real thing, the illusion of large genitals.

In the third Batman film, *Batman Forever,* both the suit and the actor playing Batman are different than the suit and actor in the previous two films. Val Kilmer replaces Keaton. It is only in the third film that the audience sees actual male flesh. Kilmer is shown without his shirt, an opportunity not offered to Keaton in either of the two previous films. Could this be because Kilmer is better looking and has a better body than Keaton?

The rubber suit in *Batman Forever* appears even harder and more inflated than it did in *Batman* and *Batman Returns*. It also comes with something new—nipples. The addition of nipples to the rubber suit makes the suit more real, easier for the audience to view Batman and Batman's body as a highly desirable sex object. There is no other reasonable explanation for the sudden addition of nipples to the Batsuit. As the film's director, Joel Schumacher, says in *Premiere* magazine, "I wanted a very sexy, very sensual, very body-hugging suit."[19]

Batman Forever was also the first of the three films to include the character of Robin, Batman's protégé and action/adventure hero in training. Batman and the Batsuit remain the masters, but Robin (Chris O'Donnell) and Robin's suit are equally hard and pumped. Even before O'Donnell becomes Robin, the audience knows that his body lives up to the expected stereotype. O'Donnell is first seen as a member of a trapeze-performing family act in a circus. While performing his act, O'Donnell wears form-fitting tights, a costume that amply displays his well-muscled body.

In *The Bridges of Madison County,* it is Clint Eastwood, a long-time symbol of sex and masculinity in Hollywood movies, who becomes the object of male display. The focus of the display, however, is not *on* his body but *about* his body.

The role of Kincaid is a major change for Eastwood. Movie audiences were used to seeing Eastwood in gun-slinging cowboy and Dirty Harry films. These were the roles and the films which presented Eastwood as the epitome of masculinity, and the roles and films which made him a Hollywood sex symbol. The role of Kincaid, as it is written in the book, is also a symbol of sex and masculinity but for different reasons than the characters Eastwood played in his previous films.

In the book, Kincaid is described as having a muscular body and therefore is considered sexually desirable.[20] Could Eastwood, a sixty-five-year-old man, live up to these descriptions and comparisons? This is where the focus shifts from being *on* Eastwood's body to being *about* Eastwood's body. "[W]hen [Eastwood] takes off his shirt," writes Rita Kempley in *The Washington Post,* ". . . it's easy to see why the love scenes take place in the dark."[21]

In the eyes of some moviegoers, Eastwood may remain a symbol of male sex and masculinity capable of playing a role such as Kincaid. However, in the eyes of Hollywood, and through the eyes of Eastwood himself, since he was the film's director, he is not sexy enough to be shown making love in a well-lit love scene.

Had the role of Kincaid been played by an actor considered more attractive and more physically appealing than Eastwood, the love scenes would have been filmed very differently. The presence, not the absence, of Kincaid's physical beauty and appeal would be the focus of the male display in the film.

Dirty Harry has gotten too old and too out of shape to be the action/adventure hero. He is still capable of falling in love and still capable of sexually satisfying a woman. Because his aged body is not something movie audiences want to look at—or a body that can not be identified with—it is best, according to Hollywood, to shroud his undesirability in darkness. In the film, Francesca, like Beauty, is able to overlook her beloved's physical appearance. Hollywood does not extend the same credit to its ticket-buying audiences.

*   *   *

Although the focus in Hollywood films on the male body as a definition or identification of masculinity may have shifted from ultramuscular to only slightly muscular, the defined or thin male body in films remains an indicator of accepted masculinity and a representation of the accepted ideal male body in American culture. This does not mean, however, that the action-hero ultramuscular body personified by Schwarzenegger and the like are disappearing from American films.

As Schwarzenegger and his Hollywood cohorts begin to age—a factor rendering them less profitable to studios and less appealing to movie audiences—Hollywood producers and filmmakers search for "fresher, younger muscle." To be eligible, these new actors must possess "great bodies" and "good looks."[22] Without meeting these qualifications—criteria obviously more important than a good script or a competent director—an action movie is destined to fail at the box office. In addition, the absence of these bodies and looks would trigger a wave of hysteria among men who derive their own definitions of masculinity and justify their own personal sense of physical appeal from the men they see on movie screens. Neither Hollywood nor the male ego could survive such a disaster.

As stereotyped male bodies continue to be a part of Hollywood films, and as male and female moviegoers continue to see and accept Hollywood male images as cultural ideals, men and their bodies are forever categorized among the best, the adequate, or the unacceptable. What results is a tier: ultramuscular bodies are best, slightly muscular bodies are adequate, overweight or otherwise out-of-shape bodies are unacceptable. Unfortunately, this tiered appraisal of the male body leaves many men primed for rejection.

Chapter 6

Body Guide: Television

Because of strict censorship guidelines and frequent threats of sponsor boycotts, network television programming and programmers have to be careful about nudity. Until recently, television did not have the advantage that films have of a ratings system intended to prevent certain viewers from watching certain films. Anyone, regardless of his or her age, parental control notwithstanding, can turn on the television set. Because of this, individual television programs, with some exceptions, are not arenas for showcasing excessive nudity, male or female. Exposed female breasts, for example, are rare—relegated to an occasional peekaboo glance on the PBS network. Displays of female bodies on network television are generally limited to women prancing about in sexy lingerie, skimpy bikinis, or towels.

Naked male chests appear in television programming because the chest is a part of the male anatomy that can be exposed without upsetting the censors or the sponsors and because the bare male chest offers the suggestion of sex. The suggestion is subtle enough to get the approval of censors and sponsors, yet blatant enough to catch and hold the viewer's attention.

If a television program is going to show a male chest, those who are producing, creating, and casting the program are going to be very particular when it comes to choosing which male chest to expose. In most cases, not just any male chest will do, since television, similar to other industries in our culture, relies on and uses current notions of accepted male beauty and male physical appearance to attract and keep viewers.

To remain competitive, network television has been forced to adopt viewer-attracting and viewer-sustaining methods that have proven successful in the film industry. Glenn Caron, a television producer, suggests, in a *New York Times* article, that male images on television are direct copies of male images in films and credits the women's movement, in part, for helping to bring about television's new man. Because, as Caron argues, in years prior to 1986, men had begun to disappear from television; he conceived "the swaggering hero" of *Moonlighting* because he was determined to put a real man back on television.[1]

Susan Faludi, author of *Backlash: The Undeclared War Against American Women*, also noticed the shifting presence between men and women on television in the 1980s. According to Faludi, the absence of female characters in television programs of the latter years of the 1980s harkened back to the 1950s and 1960s, when male characters dominated television programming. As Faludi points out, only two of the ten most highly rated television shows in the 1960 television season had recurring female characters. Faludi identifies the 1985-1986 season as a time when "women began to shrink and dwindle" from 1980s television programming. As she further notes, "An analysis of prime-time TV in 1987 found 66 percent of the 882 speaking characters were male—about the same proportion as in the '50s."[2]

In addition to ensuring successful competition with the film industry, the look and representation of men on television is important because "[w]omen have more influence in front of their sets than they do at the movies" and because "women represent not only the majority of viewers but, more important, they represent the viewers that advertisers most want to reach."[3] Because television programs are so often fantasy oriented, television producers in the 1990s have no choice but to give women what they, the producers, think women want—good-looking, sexy men.

PRIME-TIME BEEF

Male stereotypes are nothing new to network television programming. Ricky Ricardo in *I Love Lucy* was a stereotype of the 1950s male, the dominating, money-earning, and all-controlling husband. In the 1970s, Lou Grant, the quasi-chauvinistic teddy bear, ruled the WJM-TV newsroom on *The Mary Tyler Moore Show*, while Mike Brady in *The Brady Bunch* relinquished some of his control to his stay-at-home-I-have-a-housekeeper wife but remained the sole money earner. Hawkeye Pierce of *M*A*S*H* was the semisensitive, sex-on-the-brain male who managed to get the attention and bodies of attractive nurses. In the 1980s, *Miami Vice* gave us two suave, good-looking, good-bodied detectives who turned prime-time television programming into a fashion show and helped make the five o'clock shadow a national symbol of manliness. Sam Malone of *Cheers* and David Addison of *Moonlighting* symbolized good-looking men who either didn't care about or didn't quite understand feminism and women's rights. In the late 1980s, Michael Steadman of *thirtysomething* became the handsome husband devoted to his wife, his kids, and the gym. He didn't mind, not too much anyway, that his wife wanted a career outside the home. Michael epitomized the emerging new man, often confused by a male sensitivity that sometimes bordered on emasculation. Michael also became one of the first television stereotypes of the good-looking man who is equally good-hearted. He never cheated on Hope, his wife. Infidelity and the subsequent breaking up of a marriage were left up to Elliot, Michael's less sensitive, less attractive, and less muscular business partner and sidekick.

During the 1980s, men and male roles began to shift dramatically in the real world—ping-ponging between being macho and masculine to being sensitive and caring and back to being macho and masculine—so television had to accommodate by redefining the qualities of several of its male television characters. Male characters in such shows as *St. Elsewhere, Remington Steele,* and *Magnum P.I.* underwent drastic alterations. Male sensitivity came and went. Similar to men in the movies, men on television started looking for and finding more violent and more stereotypical manifestations of repressed masculinity. They took to the streets, seeking multiple sex partners and fisticuffs.[4] What men were made to be in movies and real life became what men were made to be on television. By the end of the 1980s and the beginning of the 1990s, cancellation of once popular prime-time television shows caused the Hawkeye Pierces, David Addisons, Michael Steadmans, and Sam Malones of the world to fade away into television and cultural history.

Although some of the male stereotypes of the 1950s, 1970s, and 1980s continue to exist in television programming of the 1990s, current television has added to the list its own version of the male stereotype. To remain competitive with the film industry and with the ever-expanding cable and music television industries, television programs in the 1990s are now relying on physical stereotypes of men in much the same way past television programs relied on emotional and characteristic male stereotypes. Some of today's male characters in television programs continue to be sensitive and caring, while others are scoundrels and villains. There is, however, one important difference between men on television today and men on television of past decades.

Whether today's television men are sensitized feminists or rough-hewn miscreants, their behavior is often acted out in scenes in which they are as naked as the censors and sponsors will allow them to be. Because men on television are often seen in only their boxer shorts and briefs, rather than fully dressed, their bodies need to fit within rigidly defined and universally accepted ideals of male physical beauty.

Not every program on television offers exposed male bodies, although almost any television program could be a vehicle for the exhibition of male flesh. It appears that only in certain television programs are exposed male body parts seen. Male nudity does not occur often in situation comedies, for example, although exposed male bodies have been seen in such comedies as *Murphy Brown, Wings, Roseanne, Seinfeld,* and *Caroline in the City.* The majority of programs that frequently expose male bodies are dramatic shows, sometimes referred to as prime-time or nighttime soap operas.

Male actors in television programs such as *Beverly Hills 90210, Melrose Place,* and *Party of Five,* for example, regularly are featured in scenes that call for them to remove their shirts or to be seen while wearing little clothing, and there is not an ugly or out-of-shape man among them. When unattractive or out-of-shape characters appear in these shows, usually as the bad guys, the butt of jokes, or as minor characters, it is almost a certainty that these men will remain fully dressed.

Although most television programs, dramatic or otherwise, do not completely rely on male nudity as a way to attract viewers and increase ratings, there is one show in particular that does, *Baywatch,* which stars David Hasselhoff, "the tan, tall, blue-eyed hunk who plays Mitch." According to *TV Guide*, *Baywatch* is the most-watched show in the world, claiming an audience of one billion people.[5]

Baywatch is a show about the lives and work of California lifeguards. Because of this premise, in nearly every scene, the main characters, male and female lifeguards, are seen in swimsuits. From the opening credits to the closing credits, *Baywatch* is a parade of flesh, male and female. Could this be the reason, in part, why *Baywatch* is so immensely popular? The show's star doesn't think so. David Hasselhoff claims that the show's buffed characters only account for a portion of the show's appeal to viewers. Hasselhoff also credits the success and popularity of *Baywatch* to the show's appeal to the family unit.[6] Hasselhoff's seeming hesitation to give full credit for his show's success to the presence of near-naked bodies may stem from the fact that *Baywatch* regularly features a bevy of near-naked beautiful women. If Hasselhoff, or anyone connected with the show, were to publicly proclaim the presence of female bodies as a component of the show's success, the media would turn it into an all-out declaration of female stereotyping and exploitation of women. Feminists would rally their troops and march to the border. Yet, female stereotyping and exploitation of women are exactly what *Baywatch* succeeds in doing. Few, however, will say so. Furthermore, male stereotyping and exploitation of *men's* bodies are, seemingly, ignored and unimportant.

In today's world of television programming and ratings competition, it is questionable whether a show can survive as number one in the world based solely on its appeal to the family unit. Arguably, *Baywatch* could continue to succeed if, for some reason, the cast and locale of *Baywatch* were suddenly transferred to, for example, the Midwest where it is not always warm and sunny. However, after losing the perfect excuse to have the characters continually prance around in their swimsuits and show off their beautiful and appealing bodies, the show, more than likely, would not maintain the ratings it currently holds. As *Entertainment Tonight*'s Mary Hart commented on national television, the success of *Baywatch* can be attributed to three key ingredients: "sun, sand, and especially skin." Its success can also be attributed to sex, since "sex is what *Baywatch* is all about."[7]

Serial dramas and other nighttime television shows are not the only ones exposing male flesh to television viewers. There are also entertainment news programs and tabloid news programs that frequently air segments on men and male bodies. These programs, however, are not necessarily set apart from prime-time series simply because they are reporting the news instead of making the news. Nighttime entertainment and tabloid news programs often air segments on how the advertising, film, and television industries use men's bodies to sell their products. They present their subjects as news but, in reality, end up exploiting and objectifying male bodies in exactly the same manner as the industries on which they report.

A weekend edition of *Entertainment Tonight,* a program titled *Hot Faces '95,* aired a segment on "supermodel" Michael Bergin. *Entertainment Tonight* shows Bergin's larger-than-life billboard on which he is wearing nothing but his Calvin Klein underwear. They show him posing for calendar photographs, each picture showing him more and more unclothed, until he is finally naked, holding a pair of sweatpants in front of his crotch.

Next, *Entertainment Tonight* shows Bergin auditioning for a commercial; once again he is stripped to his underwear. To end the segment, *Entertainment Tonigh*t returns to Bergin's calendar shoot, the sweatpants still strategically placed. "We just had to go back to that shot one more time for you," says Leeza Gibbons, the *Entertainment Tonight* anchorperson. The look on Gibbons' face suggests she is enjoying the second look as much as the viewers are meant to enjoy it.

Tabloid news shows, such as *Hard Copy* and *Inside Edition,* frequently use male bodies as subjects in their programs. They have aired segments on male hunk calendars and male soap opera studs posing for *Playgirl* magazine. Similar to *Entertainment Tonight,* these shows attempt to legitimize these segments by making them seem newsworthy. Again, in reality, they are nothing of the sort. They are simply cleverly conceived gimmicks to attract viewers and increase ratings.

DAYTIME HUNKS

Although the continued success and popularity of prime-time or nighttime television programming does not depend in whole on male nudity and subsequent stereotypes of male physical beauty, the same cannot be said for daytime soap operas. Finding soap operas with unattractive men cast as principal characters is difficult. Principal male characters in daytime soap operas are both the good guys and the bad guys. Unlike the good and the bad guys in movies and fiction, soap operas do not always present good guys who are attractive and bad guys who are ugly. In soap operas, an actor portraying a bad guy has as much a chance at becoming a heartthrob for soap fans as does a good guy. Consider the character Todd Manning on *One Life to Live*. A one-time rapist and all-around bad guy, Todd redeems himself by playing the part of the hero, saving the lives of two children and one woman. As a result, female fans of the program clamored for clemency and gave Todd, or rather the actor portraying him, heartthrob status. Viewers found it in their hearts to forgive Todd his acts of rape and murder. Why? Fans of *One Life to Live* consider Todd attractive and sexy. Were Todd an ugly man, he would have never been forgiven, and female fans would not crowd the studio's backdoor shouting his name.[8]

Because it is assumed that women are the primary audience of daytime television, soap operas depend heavily on the physical appearance of men in their programs. The networks, viewers, and actors know this. The actors are often quite candid on this subject. "When I got into daytime [television], I kind of realized that taking the shirt off was part of what the audience enjoys," says J. Eddie Peck of *The Young and the Restless*.[9] As with *Baywatch*, daytime soap operas would be hard-pressed to keep their high number of viewers without the tease of exposed male bodies.

Besides soap operas, daytime television is overrun with talk shows. Much has been written and said about the role of talk shows in modern culture, they are often accused by critics and viewers alike for grossly exploiting their guests.

A frequent subject on talk shows is sex and sexuality, and men and men's bodies are often offered as fare for these discussions. The *Ricki Lake Show* aired a program on men who claim to have the ability to attract any woman they desire because of their good looks. On her show, Jenny Jones offered a panel of men obsessed with their own physical attractiveness. Both Phil Donahue and Oprah Winfrey have aired shows on male body image based on a *Psychology Today* survey. Other daytime talk shows have aired similar segments, with topics ranging from obesity to male escorts. Similar to nighttime entertainment and tabloid news programs who attempt to present the male body as news, daytime talk shows exploit male good looks and self-identified desirability solely in an effort to beat out the competition and thereby remain on the air.

SINGING THE BODY FANTASTIC

Cable television is an amalgamation of several industries, a partnership of sorts between the television industry, the Hollywood and independent film industries, and the music industry. MTV, the result of a marriage between television and music, has spawned an extensive array of critical and media studies on how music videos and music celebrities have influenced popular culture.

Music videos have come a long way since MTV's beginning in 1981, going from strictly filmed concert or studio performances to highly stylized and often controversial minimovies. The music and lyrics of songs performed in music videos sometimes act as a script but just as often serve only as a background to the visuals. It is often difficult to determine what the relationship is between the music and the visuals or whether a relationship actually exists. One certainty is that music videos and MTV have changed completely how music is made and, more important, how music is sold.

Music is no longer only something to listen to; it is something to watch. The songs are no longer disembodied voices coming from stereo speakers. Because music has become a visual medium as much as, or more than, a sound medium, what musical performers look like is as important to their continued success as what they sound like.

"So what happened to all the fat guys and wimps in pop music?"[10] begins an article in *The New York Times*. In the bygone days of the recording industry, it was the voices and the music of these fat guys and wimps that made them superstars. An overweight or wimpy singer was fine in the days when maleness and masculinity were not measured in physical appearance and in the days when music came in the form of sound over the radio or stereo and not as visuals from a television screen. But, the old days are gone. Differing measures and changing definitions of maleness and masculinity have not ignored the music industry or the male performers within that industry.

If today's male musicians want success, they have more to consider than just their vocal or musical abilities.

For male musical performers to become and remain a success in today's music industry, they must have the body worthy of today's rigid standards of male appearance. As indicated by the likes of Bruce Springsteen, Axl Rose, members of the Red Hot Chili Peppers, Bobby Brown, Chris Isaak, and others, the bodies of male musical performers are increasingly expected to be muscular.[11]

Thanks to music videos and MTV, male musical performers are visual celebrities who have become models of masculinity and icons of male beauty. Their bodies become the focus of the videos in which they perform, confirming the notion that male singers can be as macho and manly as their film counterparts.[12]

Because music videos have evolved beyond videotaped concert or studio performances, background images, animate and inanimate, are essential to a video's overall look. Women and female sexuality have always been elements of pop music. Before music videos evolved into what they are currently, women were the groupies who pushed themselves against the concert stage hoping to get the attention of the male performers. What the male performers looked like was often unimportant. Rock-star status, and the money and fast-lane living that went with it, took precedence over unruly hair and beards, multiple tattoos, and beer bellies. All of this shifted, however, when music became a visual medium.

As music videos evolved, women became latex- and bikini-clad props gyrating in the background or foreground, mainly for the viewing pleasure of the male performers and the male audience. Although women continue to act out these roles in music videos, they are now joined by male props that serve the same purpose. P and A (pecs and ass) have become as popular as T and A (tits and ass) in music videos. More and more male musicians are being seen with less and less clothing in their music videos. Since viewers of music videos are as discriminating as the viewers of theatrical movies and television programs, they want videos to have male musicians and male characters who are good-looking and muscular.

Although female musical performers and their videos may not have achieved equal status with the male side of the business, women musicians and the videos of their songs have made significant inroads in the music industry. Whether it is simply a tit-for-tat measure or an acute understanding of what sells music in today's marketplace, men's bodies have become frequent and highly exposed components of videos showcasing women's music. From Madonna to Martha Wash to Melissa Etheridge to Janet Jackson, female music performers are adorning their videos with near-naked men. Whether these men are dancers cavorting around the female star or used simply as statuary, they are ornamentation; they serve as objects of accepted and desired male physical appearance that are meant to create both heterosexual and homosexual arousal.[13]

In addition to the broadcasting of music videos, MTV offers other programming in which men and men's bodies are displayed as offerings of sexual appeal and desirability. Most notable among these programs are the annual spring break broadcasts. Each year, MTV broadcasts from popular resort-type destinations where college students gather to spend their spring break vacations. In between and during concert performances of popular musical artists, the MTV cameras pan the crowd. Swimsuit-clad men appear everywhere, dancing in front of the stage or on boats anchored in nearby waters. The sun beats down on these men, bouncing off their handsome faces and sculpted bodies.

At some point in the program, MTV holds a beauty contest, during which female and male would-be beauty queens and kings prance down a runway in front of a whistling, catcalling, applauding audience. The beauty king crown is given to the man chosen by the audience as the winner—the most handsome, the most fit, and the most desirable of the male competitors. He is the perfect match for the beauty queen. Together they represent the ideal couple, a combined model of heterosexual physical perfection.

* * *

With the inclusion of cable broadcasting, and MTV in particular, television offers its viewers a continuous twenty-four-hour-per-day showing of stereotyped and culturally defined male bodies. Whenever sex—an umbrella of human desire that covers love, romance, and relationships—and men are components of television programs, there is almost total certainty that very specific types of men will be used. Whether it is daytime soap operas, nighttime soap operas, talk shows, entertainment programs, music videos, or tabloid news pro-grams, if the exposing of male flesh is part of the script or story, the male body will be no ordinary male body. Naked men in television programs are predominately white and young. Their faces are hand-some or good-looking. They generally have little or no chest hair. The muscles of their bodies, necks to calves, are gym-toned and -trained. There is rarely even a glimpse of the worst of all male deficiencies, the pot belly.

The content of television programs has been blamed for much of what is wrong with modern society and life, from increasing violence to the decline of family values. Television is a pipeline of informa-tion and ideas feeding directly into millions of American households. As more and more network, independent, and cable channels broad-cast programs that stereotype and objectify male bodies, more and more young and adult men, who do not look anything at all like the teen idols and hunks they see on television, are going to find it difficult to maintain a solid, individually defined base of self-esteem and self-confidence. More and more women and gay men are going to compare their real-life male partners to the fantasies-presented-as-realities that television offers. A television commercial for Bally's health centers sums it up: "You've seen them on TV and now you want one for yourself—a new body."

Chapter 7

Bigger Is Better:
Pornography and Erotica

Pornography is believed to be a cultural device glorifying male domination over women. It is accused of exploiting women and their bodies. It is considered a vehicle through which men learn that it is permissible to rape. It is described as an educational demonstration of how men should have sex. These are the elements and consequences of pornography argued by writers, academics, judges, lawmakers, feminists, psychologists, and the countless number of other voices attempting to interpret the roles and ramifications of pornography in our culture.

Pornography is also a tool used to teach men how to be men. Through visual images, it illustrates and showcases conceptual and/ or culturally constructed portraits of masculinity and manhood. However, more than this, pornography teaches men how to be *sexually desirable*. The issue of desirability in pornography is an important one. Pornography does not, of course, teach that women in pornography actually desire the men with whom they are shown having sex. Women's desire in pornography is a nonissue. The desirability being addressed here is that of the male viewer and how he is compared, either by himself or by others, to the men seen in pornography. This of course assumes that men—straight men—pay attention to male bodies in pornography, although it would seem difficult for them not to, given that the male body in straight pornography is as visible as the female body.

Since pornography is primarily for the sexual stimulation of men, it is possible that the men found in pornography are not required to live up to the high standards of male beauty and male physical attractiveness which are found in other areas of modern-day culture.

Despite this, however, there is an element of physical stereotyping of men and male bodies occurring in pornography that, similar to its counterparts in other areas of culture, creates an archetype of the male body which is viewed as an ideal.

Can a man watch a video of another man having sex without, in some way, comparing himself to the man on the screen? This is a difficult question to answer, most notably because straight men are traditionally silent about their impressions of the appearance of their own bodies.

Men often brag about their sexual conquests and may indeed brag about the size of their penises as it relates to these sexual conquests. The latter, however, is probably described by innuendo and not actual dimensions of length and girth. It is highly unlikely that men admit to other men the size of their penises because of the fear that other men will claim to have even larger penises. Since there are limited opportunities for straight men to be naked in front of other men and because "the naked male body continues to be a tricky matter for heterosexual men," facts of penis size are almost never given the chance to be disputed or put to the test.[1]

Since most men probably view pornography in private, completely out of sight of other men, it is impossible to know precisely what men think about while watching pornography. It can be assumed that they think of the women on the screen—I wish I had her, or I wish I were him (meaning the man on the screen who is actually having sex with a woman and not home alone masturbating). If the latter thought does occur, in what context is it to be taken? Is the man watching the video saying he wishes he were the man in the video because that man is having sex with a woman? Is he wishing he looked like that man or had a penis like that man's so he, the viewer, could actually get a beautiful woman to have sex with him?

Straight pornography is about men having sex with women. Straight pornography is not about women having sex with men, since women in pornography are there mainly for the purpose of pleasing men. When men watch video pornography they are, presumably, watching the women and what is being done to the women, without noticing the men. If they were to notice the men, their sexuality, or at least their masculinity, would be questioned immediately. But, how can men watch penises go in and out of vaginas without noticing the penises? Can men see these penises—penises that are often more than average in size—without looking down at themselves in comparison? How can men watch male bodies thrusting and gyrating above female bodies without noticing the male bodies? Can men see these bodies—bodies that are often muscular or well-defined—without looking at their own bodies in comparison? Men who watch video pornography are not equipped with special visual powers rendering the men in pornography invisible. Whether or not men who watch pornography *acknowledge* the men they see on the screen, they cannot ignore the male presence and what that male presence represents—objectifying the male body.

What exactly, then, are men seeing in the men featured in pornography? Although pornography does not have the kind of influence on people that other industries have, it does contribute, in its own way and within its own share of the male market, to cultural ideals of male beauty and male physical appearance. It does this by placing male bodies in, perhaps, the ultimate social setting—sex. Advertising, as an example, uses male bodies in sexual situations to sell a product, but actual sex is implied, not real. In advertising, the male body *represents* sex, but in pornography, the male body *has* sex and *is* sex.

The assertion made by one writer that men in pornography are not always men who can be considered attractive is not entirely accurate.[2] Although many men in straight pornography do not meet current standards of male beauty and male physical appearance, there are many pornographic films and videos that use men who have bodies which fit well within the boundaries of current stereotypes.

Because many pornographic films and videos have plots in which the viewer is led to believe the women in the films actually desire the men, it is important to producers of pornography to use real men to whom real women would be attracted sexually. The producers of these videos seem to believe that few women are sexually attracted to men who are fat or skinny.[3] There is also the belief that women who are considered attractive in our society are beyond the reach of most men.[4] Since the fantasy presented in pornography is that real sexual desire does indeed exist between the men and women in these films, pornography does play a role in the sexual socialization of men. Men who view pornography are being told and shown that to be the object

of desire they must look like the men they see on the screen. Otherwise, their fantasies may be forever unfulfilled, and they may never
know true sexual satisfaction.

If body type does not make a difference in straight pornography,
then we would see even more overweight or out-of-shape or otherwise undesirable men in the videos. Given the argument that women's
desire in pornography is moot, why be concerned at all with the
appearance of men in pornographic materials? One possible answer
is that producers of pornography are trying to create the illusion of
women's desire and are assuming, based on current trends of male
appearance, that women want to have sex with men who are muscular, handsome, and well-endowed.

Straight pornography offers the viewer clear examples of stereotyped maleness and masculinity that go well beyond the theory that
men are dominant because they are men. If bodily image were not a
component of defined and/or stereotyped masculinity, there would be
no regard to bodily appearance in pornography. Then, and only then,
could producers of pornography feel free to use *any* type of male
body in their products. However, this is not the case, as any thorough
examination of pornography reveals. Could it be then that body type
and body appearance do make a difference in straight pornography?
To some extent, they do, although certainly not as much as in gay
male or bisexual pornography.

Pornography aimed at bisexual and gay men is very specific about
male body type. Whereas straight pornography can suggest that no
specific body type is preferred, this is not the case in bisexual and
gay pornography. Gay male fantasies do not allow room for out-of-
shape bodies, small penises, or ugly faces. The same is true for
bisexual fantasies in which two men are with one woman. The equiv-
alent of this situation in straight pornography is very different. In
straight pornography, when two men are having sex with one woman
at the same time, the men never touch each other and, presumably,
have no interest in each other's bodies. Whenever two men are
together for the purpose of having sex with each other, whether or
not a woman is present, the bodies of these men will always fit
within the belief that the mesomorphic body type is preferred over all
other types.

Straight men who do not have muscular bodies, who are over- or underweight, who do not have above-average penises, or who are otherwise considered sexually unattractive and/or sexually undesirable are led to believe they stand little chance of attracting the type of women seen in pornography. In real-life social situations related to the search for sexual partners, unattractive men are the least likely to be sexually successful. They may possess other stereotypical characteristics of masculinity—money and power, for example—but without the accompanying stereotypical body, their chances of having consensual sex with attractive, desirable women are severely handicapped. Moreover, men who see the women in pornography as the ultimate or ideal sexual partner, and who believe themselves to be good catches despite their pot bellies or other qualifying body disorders may not even realize why they are being denied sex with a desired partner. If indeed they are not consciously comparing their own bodies to those of men in pornography, their sexual rejection by women becomes a mystery and possibly a source of misogynist tendencies and behavior.

It is difficult to know if and how male bodies will change in straight pornography. Whether or not the pornography industry decides to play catch up with other industries within our culture and begin placing greater importance on male physical appearance cannot be known. Answering this question will take a continuing look at men and male bodies in pornography in the years ahead.

It will also take more research to know fully how and to what extent the appearance of male bodies, as they appear in pornographic materials, influences male insecurity. Most research and studies of pornography as a source of male characteristics and behavior have focused on issues of misogyny and antiwomen behavior. Moreover, most of the information available with regard to how straight men react to male bodies in pornography focuses on penis size.

As one writer noted about pornography, "To bring themselves into relationship with an objectified female body, males must objectify their own bodies as well."[5] This writer argues that a relationship exists between pornography's perpetuation of the notion that women are always available and the notion that men are always ready. What results is male anger directed toward women because women in real-life situations are not like women in pornography. The notion that men are always ready, willing, and able to have sex—which in reality is not completely accurate—creates insecurity in men because they do not match the standards of penis size evident in pornography.[6] This, however, assigns men's insecurity to penis size alone and makes the penis the sole source of male sexual pleasure and the one body part most important to men and women. It assumes that straight men do notice penises in pornography and that men can be made to feel insecure about the size of their own penises. The notion that men do care about penis size can only be assumed because no study or research has ever given definitive evidence on the subject. A recent survey in *Psychology Today* asked men if they *believed* penis size to be important *to women*. The survey did not ask *men* how *they* feel about penis size.[7]

If men can be made to feel insecure with regard to penis size in pornography can they then be made to feel insecure about their overall body appearance based upon what they see in pornography?

In a checklist of the effects pornography can have on men, the group Men Against Pornography includes the following as one of the statements on the list: "You become dissatisfied with your own physical appearance and/or sexual expression."[8] When a men's group imposes this possibility onto other men, it is apparent that the appearance of male bodies in pornography is not going unnoticed by men. As a result, one has to wonder about women. Do they notice men's bodies in pornography?

THE MALE CENTERFOLD

Pornographic material created for women and women's sexual enjoyment is extremely limited when compared to pornography created for men and men's sexual enjoyment. Women may choose to view pornography that is intended generally for a male audience, but pornography created exclusively for women does not exist in the numbers it does for men. Instead, women have what is generally regarded as erotica.

Although there are many women's magazines, very few of them offer women anything more than implied sex or a peek at a sexy, and often quite naked, model in advertisements. The only true erotic magazine existing for women is *Playgirl*. *Playgirl* is a magazine of pinups, similar to its male counterparts *Playboy* and *Penthouse*. The difference in *Playgirl*, of course, is that the pinups are of naked men instead of naked women.

According to writer Margaret Walters, a female pinup "is endlessly fascinating because she is elusive—because no woman can ever achieve that ideal femininity and no man truly possess it."[9] This has always been the criticism of how women are depicted in magazines such as *Playboy* and *Penthouse*. Is it fair, then, to criticize *Playgirl* for the same thing?

The men who are being photographed for *Playgirl* are being treated no differently than *Playboy* bunnies or *Penthouse* pets. The men are there solely for the sexual titillation of women, creating fantasies of the ideal male sexual partner and placing an incredible amount of pressure on men to live up to the standards of male beauty espoused by *Playgirl*.

In *Playgirl*, the roles of sexism and sexists are reversed. Women are given the opportunity to look at men merely as playthings—but not any plaything will do. The men in *Playgirl* are as stereotyped as they are in other areas of our culture. *Playgirl* offers "photo spreads of the most gorgeous guys on earth," according to the magazine's subscription blurb, and features naked men posed in various locations, in much the same way women are posed in *Playboy* and *Penthouse*. In *Playgirl*, we find naked male models who are fishing, playing pinball, getting their hair shampooed, chopping firewood, cooking, and hiking. Typical copy in a *Playgirl* table of contents describes men as being "delectable" and "sizzling."

Readers, who are presumably female, are encouraged to send in photographs of the men in their lives, with a chance at having the photograph published under the title "Real Men: Does your man have what it takes?"

In an end-of-the-year issue, *Playgirl* readers are asked to vote for the "Man of the Year." Twelve photos of the previous year's centerfolds are printed, and readers are instructed to choose one man as the winner. Is all of this to be taken seriously, or is it merely considered cute because it is, after all, only photographs of naked men and not photographs of naked women?

If a woman is photographed hiking naked through the woods or in the kitchen wearing only a chef's cap or playing pinball, and the photographs are printed in magazines marketed to men, the often presumed result is the degradation of women. Yet, when men are photographed naked in similar poses and printed in a magazine marketed to women, we hear little about the degradation of men. What we hear instead is that women are fighting back by putting men in roles traditionally reserved for women. It is called reverse sexism and is meant to be a counterattack against a male-dominated society. In truth, however, it creates a double standard. It gives women permission to objectify men and male bodies under the pretense that if it is acceptable for men to degrade women then the reverse is true also.

Who are the women reading (looking at) *Playgirl?* Are they any different from the men who read (look at) *Playboy* and *Penthouse?* Are the men sexist pigs, while the women are only getting even?

If letters to the editors are any indication of what type of women are reading and looking at *Playgirl,* it is clear that women like what they see: "Every inch of his body is pure perfection."[10] "I have never seen a man so handsome and a body so fantastic."[11] "He's truly a 'work of art.'"[12]

Women who read *Playgirl* also make a distinction between photographs of naked men as entertainment and photographs of naked men as something more. The claim has been made that the photographs in *Playgirl* are not pornography but simply photographs of naked men.[13] Many say the same about *Playboy* and *Penthouse*— yet they are fiercely attacked since these two magazines show photographs of naked women. Again, similar depictions of naked men does not promote the same argument or debate.

Some will argue that *Playgirl* magazine deserves its place in society. Women are more likely to be the proponents of this argument because *Playgirl* allows women the chance to assume the rare role of having power over men. Men's bodies become to women what women's bodies are to men. It is unlikely, however, that men are threatened by *Playgirl*'s presence. It appears that men will always be the kings of pornography, and *Playgirl* alone will not dethrone them. Yet *Playgirl* does play a role in stereotyping men's bodies and the manipulation and exploitation of male sexuality, much more so than pornography aimed at straight men. Some straight men who view pornography probably do not care what men's bodies look like and how men's bodies are used in sex. *Playgirl* obviously does care and believes that women (or gay men, at least) care; its existence depends on this.

The power women may feel while flipping through the pages of *Playgirl* cannot be very fulfilling. The reversal of a long-standing male-dominated power structure is very limited and certainly is not achieved through the publication of one erotic magazine marketed to women. While women look at *Playgirl* in the privacy of their homes, feeling fortified against male domination, outside in the real world they are being soundly defeated. Lying in bed while looking at photographs of naked men does nothing for the equality of the sexes. Turning men into playthings and sex objects hurts men and does nothing to stop the hurt being inflicted upon women. As long as women, or men for that matter, think it permissible to objectify men solely as a response to similar objectifying of women, no ground is being gained, and no one is winning.

*   *   *

Whether pornography is aimed at men or at women, men's bodies are being stereotyped by the pornography industry. If our society were ever to become one that allowed sex and sexual materials to be more publicly expressed and available, we would undoubtedly see the same type and frequency of male stereotyping in pornography as we see in other areas of our culture. Certainly, the power of the advertising, film, and television industries to influence standards of beauty and physical attractiveness—female and male—is due to their visibility and their existence in our everyday lives. Pornography does not have this type or frequency of exposure; it is limited by issues of morality and ethics in ways that advertising, film, and television are not. This does not mean, however, that pornography is not without *some* influence on standards of beauty and physical attractiveness. If pornography had no effect, it would not be surrounded by controversy, and there would not be the enormous amount of material that has been, and will be, written about the pornography industry.

Certainly, there are issues of pornography far more important and compelling than the stereotyping of male bodies. Does pornography incite men to rape women? The stereotyping and objectifying of female bodies plays a part in both asking and answering this question. Current and historical discussions about the influence of pornography on society focus mainly on how women and their bodies are being portrayed in pornography, what is being done to women's bodies in pornography, how women are made to feel about their bodies in real life, and how men are supposed to treat women's bodies in real life. Few discussions are taking place concerning how pornography makes men feel about *their* bodies. Ignoring the possibility that stereotypes of male bodies in pornography can contribute to male sexual insecurity, which may in turn lead to acts of sexual aggression toward women, is a danger that should be avoided. Women are not the only ones being hurt by pornography, and the treatment of women in pornography is only half the problem. Likewise, the changing or the eradication of the use of women and the female body in pornography is only half the solution.

Chapter 8

Skin and Bones:
Dieting and Eating Disorders

It can rightfully be argued that the culturally imposed idea "to be thin is to be beautiful" has contributed greatly to the high number of women who participate in diet programs. More than likely, there is not a day that passes by when women are forced to look at and critique their bodies. They see magazine covers, television commercials, and a plethora of television talk shows, all of which pound into their heads a very loud and clear message: WOMEN MUST BE THIN TO BE BEAUTIFUL. In more than one Jenny Craig commercial, newly thin women with tears in their eyes are shown hugging the company's namesake and offering a benediction for making them beautiful. Photographs are flashed on the screen, indicating to viewers that these now thin and beautiful women were once fat and ugly. Men are there too, although we never see them crying (that would be unmanly). However, the men are no less grateful than the women. They too are newly thin, newly sexy, newly desirable. With a little help from Jenny Craig or Weight Watchers and not-so-few dollars, men can now look like those men on the covers of *Gentlemen's Quarterly*, *Esquire*, or *Men's Health*, in the shaving products and beer commercials, or on the television talk shows who silently shout a very clear message: MEN MUST BE MUSCULAR TO BE BEAUTIFUL.

As too many women now know, an obsession with weight reduction, dieting, and looking thin can easily lead to serious eating disorders, such as anorexia and bulimia.

With the exception of scientific and academic journals and eating- or dieting-oriented publications, very little attention is paid to men who suffer from eating disorders. It is difficult to identify the reason for this. It could be argued that men who suffer from eating disorders do not seek treatment because they are afraid to be thought of as having a woman's disease. Perhaps, it is simply that the medical, psychological, and research communities do not consider the comparatively small number of men with eating disorders substantial enough to warrant extensive investigation. Whatever the reasons may be, there is no doubt that men do suffer from eating disorders, and there is no evidence suggesting that the number of men with these illnesses will decrease in the years ahead.

No agreement can be reached on how many men suffer from eating disorders. The National Association of Anorexia Nervosa and Associated Disorders estimates that one million men suffer from some sort of eating disorder. A report in *Weight Watchers Magazine* states that men account for approximately 10 percent of all anorexia and bulimia cases.[1] The introduction to *The Course of Eating Disorders* tells us that in a "Johns Hopkins experience . . . approximately 1 in 10 patients with an eating disorder has been male," while another study "disagree[s] with this number and suggest[s] a lower ratio of 1-5% of cases being male."[2] A 1992 survey of 1982 Harvard graduates, reported in *Newsweek,* found that although the number of women with eating disorders dropped the number of men suffering from eating disorders actually doubled. A 1994 study "of 131 Cornell University lightweight football players . . . found that 40 percent engaged in 'dysfunctional eating patterns' . . . with 10 percent classified as having outright eating disorders."[3]

Similar confusion reigns in attempting to identify the causes of eating disorders in men. Are the causes psychological or sociological or both? No one, it seems, can provide definitive answers, although there is much speculation. *Weight Watchers Magazine* reports that anorexia may develop during the teenage years as a means of response to family difficulties. It is also suggested that male eating disorders occur when the effects of puberty cause young boys to reduce their food intake to postpone the process of growing up. There is also the suspicion that eating disorders exist among adult males who were obese children. In this same report, the cause of bulimia in men is attributed to the very broad possibility that this illness "stems from a severe lack of self-esteem."[4]

According to A. E. Andersen, a leading researcher in eating disorders in men, other possible reasons for these illnesses in men include dieting to be more attractive to potential gay partners, being teased as a child for being fat, or a "fear of fatness and distortion of body image."[5]

Many believe that eating disorders in men are limited to certain subsets within the male population. One such subset is gay males. A study published in 1993 concludes "that, in general, homosexual males and heterosexual females showed greater actual concerns with appearance, weight, and dieting, and were perceived to possess greater body image disturbance and dieting concerns compared to heterosexual males and homosexual females."[6] The study cites previous findings which it noted that perhaps as many as 33 percent of the men who have eating disorders are gay. Although the study identifies "cultural and societal forces including the mass media and weight loss and health club industries" as links to women and eating disorders and that "most of the[se] media messages are directed towards women," it fails to identify similar messages aimed at gay men. The study fails to correlate the linking of these forces between straight women and gay men by claiming there are "very few advertisements" aimed at gay men.[7] This statement is inaccurate and incomplete because it is, presumably, referring to mainstream or nongay advertisements and does not allow for advertisements in gay-oriented publications. Furthermore, it does not account for the enormous visibility of perceived stereotypes of male beauty in nearly *all* aspects of gay male culture. Gay men, similar to straight women, cannot ignore the strong belief that to be socially and sexually acceptable they must live up to culturally imposed ideas of beauty and physical attractiveness. If members of either of these two groups do not meet these criteria, they are rejected more often than they are accepted. It is no wonder, then, that women and gay men are considered high-risk groups for developing eating disorders.

In addition to certain subsets of the population being at risk, it is believed that certain occupations and the desire to perform well within those occupations can trigger the onset of eating disorders in men. A psychologist quoted in *Psychology Today* believes that men who are "boxers, male models and wrestlers" are "among those at greatest risk."[8] Others, particularly men in the entertainment and sports industries, are also at risk, according to an article in *Weight Watchers Magazine*.[9] Notice that male models and entertainers are thrown in with the jockeys, boxers, and athletes. These are all professions that put men in the public eye, and the public eye does not want to see out-of-shape boxers, athletes, male models, and entertainers. Success within these occupations comes down to physical appearance. It seems reasonable to assume that physical ability is more important than physical appearance for jockeys, boxers, and athletes, but this is not entirely true. Certainly, physical ability is important during the course of their athletic careers. When the athletic career is over, however, they look to product promotion and endorsement to earn a living. Success in this second career is highly dependent on physical appearance because it is then that athletes cease to be athletes and become celebrities.

Other reports, however, show that men who are not jockeys, actors, or models also are susceptible to eating disorders: A fourteen-year-old boy developed an eating disorder after he gained weight and was no longer the thinnest in his school. A twenty-six-year-old male was hospitalized ten times over an eight-year period and at one time tried to kill himself by taking an overdose of aspirin. Another twenty-six-year-old male had been overweight when young and the recipient of an onslaught of teasing.[10] A twenty-one-year-old male used depression to explain his hospital stays because he believed depression was a more masculine illness than an eating disorder.[11] A twenty-five-year-old male college student was hospitalized for the first of eleven times when his weight dropped to eighty-four pounds.[12] A nineteen-year-old male told his doctor he wanted to diet in a way that would enhance muscle growth, all in an effort to have a body like Marky Mark's.[13]

One finding many studies do share is the expectation of a rise in the numbers of men who suffer from eating disorders. In a *Psychology Today* article, Steven Romano, MD, says he believes male anorexics are "very tied" to female anorexics. Just as a thin woman can look in the mirror and see herself as being overweight, so too can a man. "[T]hese males are well muscled but . . . [continue to judge] themselves by the ideal projected in the media."[14]

Perhaps the only way to stop a perceived increase in the number of men susceptible to eating disorders is to pay no attention to, and then all-out reject, culturally imposed stereotypes of the ideal male body. However, this rejection is not easy because so many are of the opinion that men are not in as much danger as women in regard to stereotyped body image. A. E. Andersen's assertion that men are not under the same societal pressures as women to be thin is inaccurate.[15] There *is* tremendous pressure placed on men to be thin (along with other physical characteristics). The covers of men's magazines are full of headlines promoting the hard fact that thinness and fitness are mandatory for today's man: "Get a Super Waistline Fast!"; "Build a Mighty Chest"; "Powerfully Fit"; "New Ways to Get Leaner, Faster, Stronger"; "Rock Hard, Right Now." Advertisements within these magazines give the same instructions. More and more frequently, newspapers and other periodicals are devoting space to articles on the changing awareness of the male figure. Billboards go up in New York City with gargantuan well-built male bodies displayed as the ultimate look. Television commercials use reverse sexism—a perverse exploitation of both men and women— and place naked or near-naked well-built men in the scrutinizing gaze of female and male onlookers.

What will it take for us to realize, fully and consciously, that men *are* suffering from eating disorders? How many more men will these diseases claim as victims before we understand that what causes eating disorders in women also causes them in men? Despite the estimated 8 million women already suffering from eating disorders, there are no clear answers, no clear directions for these women to find the help they rightfully need and deserve. Obviously then, a mere one million men is not enough. Will we have to wait until another seven million men are diagnosed before male eating disorders are taken seriously?

Because white patriarchal dogma continues to control the definition, and subsequent admission and treatment, of societal ills, eating disorders are likely to remain at or near the bottom of the list of national problems. Because of the dual perception that eating disorders affect women and are increasingly present in only certain subsets of men, gay men in particular, these illnesses are virtually ignored. It appears these eating disorders will gain the attention they rightfully deserve only when they strike white, heterosexual, middle- and upper-class men. There is a warning here that should be heeded:

Remember, a national drug problem was not recognized as such while it affected only black urban communities; AIDS was not recognized as a national epidemic while it struck only the gay male community. Many men are at risk of succumbing to eating disorders. How many of them will perish before something is done?

Chapter 9

The Unkindest Cut of All: Cosmetic Surgery

The American Society of Plastic and Reconstructive Surgeons reports that out of 696,904 total cosmetic surgery procedures performed in 1996 11 percent, or nearly 74,000, were on men. The American Academy of Cosmetic Surgery reports that, in 1990, men accounted for 30 percent of its members' cosmetic surgery procedures, a 10 percent increase over the past four years.[1] By 1994, it was estimated that one out of every four cosmetic surgeries was performed on men.[2]

Men choose to undergo cosmetic surgery for many different reasons: boost self-confidence, compete with younger men, increase their chances of getting a job, appear more trustworthy, pump up a deflated self-image, and live up to the assumption that women expect men to be better looking. Although these reasons appear to vary, the common denominator is that what men look like is crucial to emotional, social, and professional success.[3]

Cosmetic surgery is big business—a 300-million-dollar industry.[4] It exists exclusively as a beauty caterer that provides a service to whet the appetites of men and women who hunger for a quick and easy chance to look better. Even reconstructive plastic surgery performed to correct a physical disfiguration, resulting from an accident or a birth defect, continues to be cosmetic in that these procedures are performed to return the individual to a more normal appearance, which is to appear more attractive. An individual whose appearance has been in some way altered in an accident or in birth is not considered attractive and therefore must submit to surgery to correct a disfigured or defective physical appearance. Unattractiveness is reconstructed to be attractiveness, regardless of whether it is induced by an accidental disfiguration, a birth defect, or a mere desire to be more beautiful.

Cosmetic surgery has become a quick fix for a culturally defined idea of a physically inferior male. Michelangelo conceived his ideal male form when he sculpted his statue *David*. Today, cosmetic surgeons are re-creating this conceived ideal through surgery, replacing the chisel and block of marble with a scalpel and the human body. Modern-day Davids roam the world with scars on their skin and bodies replete with artificial implants.

Advertisements for cosmetic surgery centers tease men with evocative photographs of muscular men, the "afters" who are meant to represent the physical results of cosmetic surgery. "Who says you can't have this?" reads one ad copy. "This" of course is the physically perfect body. "Your face is a precious asset," reads another ad. Because the word cosmetic may not appeal to a lot of men and because the word surgery may scare them, cosmetic surgeons create more friendly and less frightening terms for their ads. Cosmetic surgery becomes facial and body *sculpture* or even *liposculpture*.

POPULAR PROCEDURES

The most popular surgical procedures chosen by men include hair replacement, nose reshaping, liposuction, eyelid surgery, collagen injections, facelifts, dermabrasion, cheek implants, ear pinning, chin augmentations, and chemical peels.[5] In addition to these, other procedures are gaining in popularity; namely, pectoral and calf implants, penile augmentation, and even gluteal implants.

Regardless of which procedure is chosen, they all require an assault on the flesh. Incredibly, these attacks are voluntary, not made necessary as a result of an accident or birth defect. Following are descriptions of some of the surgical procedures that men endure to improve or correct their physical appearance.

Hair transplant or *hair restoration* procedures involve skin grafts, scalp flaps, or scalp reduction. A graft is performed by removing a piece of skin, with hair follicles intact, from one part of the scalp and then transferring it to a bald portion of the scalp. Before the transfer is made, the bald patch is removed and discarded. A flap transplant is done by cutting a portion of the scalp, also with hair intact, and leaving one end of the flap attached. The flap is then turned until it covers the portion of the bald scalp that has again been cut away and discarded. Scalp reduction is exactly what it implies. The scalp is reduced by slicing away a portion of the bald scalp and then pulling the two edges of skin toward each other, bringing the hair closer together.

One of the most popular cosmetic surgery procedures for men (and women) is *liposuction*. An incision is made in the area of the body where the suction is to take place. Next, a tube is inserted into the body, a machine is turned on, and fat cells, along with blood from broken blood vessels, are literally sucked out of the body.

Chin reshaping is done by making a three- to four-inch incision inside the lower lip. After lifting the tissues, the chinbone is pulled free of the flesh. Using an electric saw, the surgeon cuts the bone to the desired shape and then reinserts the chinbone back into the skin.

Chemical peels are performed using a variety of chemical solutions. Depending on what type of peel is done, these chemicals include glycolic acid, lactic acid, trichloroacetic acid, salicylic acid, or carbolic acid (phenol). The chemicals are applied to the face, and when a wound appears, the skin is peeled off to expose a secondary layer.

Dermabrasion and *dermaplaning* are two additional procedures performed on facial skin. Dermabrasion procedures are done with a round metal brush, smoothing out scars and lines. In a dermaplaning, scarred skin is stripped away using an instrument called a dermatome.

Whereas the above surgical procedures in one way or another take away a piece of a man's body, artificial implants are used to add to the body, give it more definition, and make it more aesthetically appealing.[6]

Pectoral implants are tear-shaped pieces of solid silicone placed behind the chest wall. The implants are forced through an incision made in the armpit.[7]

Calf implants are performed in much the same manner as pectoral implants. An incision is made behind the knee, allowing the surgeon to open up a pocket below the fascia (the covering over the muscle), where the silicone implants are then inserted.

One implant surgery gaining in popularity is the *gluteal implant.* Through an incision made at the top of the buttock, one-inch-thick implants are inserted to lift the buttocks in much the same way as women's breasts are lifted.[8]

A type of cosmetic surgery becoming more popular is penis enlargement. *Penile augmentation* is performed to either expand the girth or length of the penis. In an operation to broaden the circumference of the penis, abdominal fat is removed by liposuction and added to the penis or grafted fat tissues from another part of the body are transferred to the penis.[9]

To surgically lengthen the penis, some of the ligaments connecting the penis to the abdominal wall are cut. Severing the ligaments allows the penis to hang lower. To ensure that the severed ligaments do not reattach themselves, the patient is instructed to "exercise" the penis by repeatedly stretching the shaft during the recovery period.[10]

WHAT PRICE BEAUTY?

The descriptions of these procedures are horrifying in their own right, but they represent only half of the full story. A complete understanding of male cosmetic surgery requires an examination of the associated risks of the procedures.

No surgery is without risk. Whereas some surgery is necessary and should not be avoided, cosmetic surgery does not fall within this category. Hair transplants, liposuction, chemical peels and dermabrasion, pectoral and calf implants, and penile augmentation are not necessary operations. Certainly the risks are not necessary. However, men apparently are not concerned with the risks, although risks associated with cosmetic surgery are very real and should not be ignored.

Hair transplant surgery often causes the scalp to bleed and scab after the procedure is performed, and scarring is common. "A scalp flap may leave a wide scar at the back of your head, making your hair thin."[11] In this case, a man can have a scar *and* thin hair, leaving one to wonder why he would choose hair transplant surgery in the first place. A man who did undergo hair transplant surgery stated that his surgery made him feel more "normal," which can only mean that baldness or thin hair made him feel abnormal. Another man who claimed his thinning hair made him look "ineffective" noted that hair transplant surgery made a "big improvement" in his self-confidence.[12]

It must be noted that advertisements for hair restoration never tell men about the risks and complications associated with hair transplant surgery. What the advertisements do say is that being bald or having thin hair is unattractive and that having a full head of hair will lead to a successful sex life. One advertisement reads, "Get hair, get babes." Another one reads, "Hair Loss in America, a Growing Crisis." In 1994, nearly 200,000 men had hair transplant or replacement surgeries.[13]

Reading about the side effects and complications associated with liposuction is akin to having a biological nightmare. The area of the body where the liposuction is performed can swell. The skin can become irritated and discolored. Fluid can accumulate, causing blood clots. Fat can collect in the bloodstream and lodge in the brain or lungs, which can result in death. *Muscle & Fitness* magazine warns us, "What you don't often hear about liposuction is that . . . recovery is often prolonged and painful."[14]

Swelling, irritation, discoloration, and blood clots are a small price to pay, it seems, when liposuction can improve the appearance of the body. According to the American Society of Plastic and Reconstructive Surgeons, 12,184 liposuction procedures in 1996 were performed on men, nearly double the number of men who had this procedure in 1992.[15] Numbers given by the American Academy of Cosmetic Surgery indicate that in 1994, 37,743 men had liposuction procedures.[16]

A man in his early thirties had liposuction to remove his "love handles." As a result, the skin on the area became looser, simply replacing one unattractive quality with another, leaving the man still dissatisfied with his physical appearance.[17] A second surgical procedure would be required to remove the loose skin, producing a noticeable scar.

In another instance involving liposuction, a seventeen-year-old boy died. Although his death was actually caused by the anesthesia, the tragedy was what brought him to the operating table in the first place. This boy thought he was overweight and received permission from his parents to undergo liposuction before his high school graduation ceremony. If it were not for society's inability to accept the obese as people and not objects to be rejected and ridiculed, this seventeen-year-old boy would still be alive today. The death of this boy is not an isolated event. The American Society of Plastic and Reconstructive Surgery has documented eleven liposuction-related deaths since the procedure was started in America in 1982.[18]

Chin reshaping can result in nerve damage, numbing the chin and lower teeth for as long as a year.[19] Chin augmentations on men accounted for 24 percent (1,139) of all such procedures performed in 1996, according to numbers issued by the American Society of Plastic and Reconstructive Surgeons.[20]

A common side effect of chemical peels is the alteration of skin color. In her book *The Complete Book of Cosmetic Surgery,* Elizabeth Morgan offers a warning: "The chemical phenol is potentially dangerous and can cause such problems as convulsions if it reaches a toxic level in your body."[21] Phenol is defined in *Webster's New Collegiate Dictionary* as a "caustic poisonous crystalline acidic compound present in coal tar and wood tar that in dilute solution is used as a disinfectant." Rough skin and fine wrinkles on the face, because they are considered unattractive, are killed in the same way germs are killed on bathroom tiles. *Men's Health* magazine reports that a new chemical is being used, trichloroacetic acid (defined in *Webster's New Collegiate Dictionary* as "a strong vesicant pungent acid used in weed control and in medicine as a caustic and astringent"), which "causes no skin lightening and less pain than older chemicals."[22] More than 2,500 men had chemical peels in 1996.[23] Though by 1994 the number of men who had chemical peels was 36,290, according to the American Academy of Cosmetic Surgery.[24]

A California plastic surgeon suggests that the pectoral implant has become popular because it changes "the body to fit accepted norms."[25] After the operation, the patient's chest is wrapped for a week. Opinions vary on how much time is needed for recovery. In *The Washington Post,* Martha Sherrill writes that a patient can resume chest exercise after six weeks.[26] *Muscle & Fitness* magazines tells us that only three weeks are needed for recovery.[27]

Because of the "equal-opportunity implant," flat-chested men, similar to small-breasted women, no longer have to be anything less than above average. Flat-chested men can stop hiding their bodies in shame. "Now men who feel their chests are a valley of humiliation can change all that with a set of surgically implanted silicone pecs." Because a well-shaped chest is so highly prized,[28] pectoral implants are glamorized by cosmetic surgeons and journalists who cite faulty genetics, old age, and lack of time as reasons enough to build a better chest, and body, through surgery.[29]

Since the Food and Drug Administration has never conducted a study on pectoral implants, long-term effects remain unknown. Men are blindly risking the odds despite recent revelations of complications associated with female breast implants. Even though pectoral implants are solid silicone (instead of the silicone gel found in female breast implants) and pose no hazard of leakage, they and the surgery are not without risks and possible complications. Dr. Mel Bircoll, a Southern California plastic surgeon, says that pectoral implants pose "very little risk" and "in general are thought to be safe."[30] This implies that *some* risk exists, and the fact that pectoral implants are *thought* to be safe reduces the risk to mere speculation. Infections and bleeding can also occur.[31] Also, the implant can slip, requiring a second operation and an additional risk to correct the misplaced silicone.

The most common problem associated with widening the penis is that a good portion of the injected fat is reabsorbed by the body. As a result, the artificial increase in girth can shrink from 35 to 50 percent. The only possible way to regain the loss is to have the penis-widening surgery repeated. An article in *Men's Health* magazine warns men that widening the penis through surgery can also cause the penis to become "irregular," creating a "cellulite-like effect."[32]

Most doctors consider penis-lengthening augmentations to be major surgery that comes with major risks. The risks include nerve damage that could prevent ejaculation or cause impotence. The operation could also result in bleeding and the possibility of infection. In addition, surgically lengthening the penis can affect the rigidity and stability of an erection.[33]

Despite the risks, more than 1,000 penile augmentation procedures are performed each year on men.[34] One California doctor claims he performs an average of 125 penis enhancement surgeries per month.[35]

These are only *some* of the known risks associated with a few of the cosmetic surgery procedures available to men. Because there is little concern over risks associated with male cosmetic surgery, the real damage, short- and long-term, may not be known for years or even decades to come. It is entirely possible that sometime a man who has had cosmetic surgery may indeed experience some sort of physical ailment or disfunction that, in the end, will be traced back to a pectoral implant, a penile augmentation, or some other such type of cosmetic surgery. Then he, and we, will see whether the result of the surgery was worth the risk.

*   *   *

"Cosmetic surgery is not 'cosmetic,' and human flesh is not 'plastic,'" writes Naomi Wolf.[36] This is a statement that cannot be ignored, whether it is applied to women or men. However, cosmetic surgery is not about human flesh at all (except in the sense that cosmetic surgery destroys human flesh); it is about surgeons' profits and society's exaggerated ideas of self-image and self-worth.

Since cosmetic surgery is a 300-million-dollar industry, there is no question that cosmetic surgeons profit by exploiting images and ideas of beauty. Liposuction procedures can cost anywhere from $1,500 to $4,000 and are performed by a single surgeon at the rate of several per day. A simple mathematical calculation reveals the amount of money being pocketed by surgeons who perform liposuction operations. Other cosmetic procedures are just as costly. An advertisement for a cosmetic surgery center in San Francisco lists the following procedures, along with the associated costs: facial peel, $1,000; face-lift and neck-lift, $3,600; collagen injection, $300; eyelid surgery, $2,100; and nose implant, $2,000.

A man's body spruced up by cosmetic surgery is no more valuable than it was before the surgery. The difference lies in whether we value the human body itself or merely the appearance of the human body. Clearly society values the look more than the body itself. Television commercials tell us "image is everything." Because of this notion, men are willing to spend large amounts of money to force their faces and bodies to conform to accepted norms.[37]

Although it is true that cosmetic surgeons sell images and ideas of beauty through their advertisements and then through their surgical procedures, cosmetic surgeons cannot be held completely responsible, if at all, for the value society places on beauty. Cosmetic surgeons provide a service that is in demand. Men (or culture in general) must assume part of the responsibility.

Cosmetic surgeons are not *forcing* men to have cosmetic surgery. Men are *volunteering* for the procedures because they believe what society is telling them about what is and is not considered an appropriate male physical appearance. The danger lies in the creation of a warped sense of self-worth. "The surgery market is imaginary," writes Naomi Wolf, "since there is nothing wrong with women's faces or bodies that social change won't cure."[38] With men, however, social change has made the male cosmetic surgery market very real. The very social change that Wolf names as a cure for the wrongs against women's faces and bodies has brought about the same wrongs against men's faces and bodies. There was a time when a man's appearance was not a criterion in assessing his worth. This is no longer true.

"Cosmetic surgery is a powerful psychological aid to being that *new you*, to start fresh."[39] What was wrong with the old you? Maybe you were bald or had a small chin, love handles, a flat chest, or a penis you considered too small. None of these are wrong, and there is no reason for them to be corrected or made better through cosmetic surgery.

When men claim that cosmetic surgery is a way to improve self-image or self-confidence, they continue to condition or qualify their opinion of themselves based on what others, or society, think of them. If a man says he *feels* better because a face-lift, for example, makes him *look* better, he is still conforming to an idealized image of what his appearance should be. He feels better only because he is told he looks better.

True self-image cannot exist if it does not originate from, and thrive on, the self. Positive self-image or heightened self-confidence are not created in men with face-lifts and penile augmentation any more than they are created in women with tummy tucks and breast implants.

Chapter 10

The Fitness Fallacy: Muscles

There are approximately 25,000 health clubs in the United States. *Muscle & Fitness* magazine has 600,000 subscribers.[1] Twenty-five million Americans do some sort of bodybuilding or weight lifting.[2]

Some will argue that the increase in male membership at gyms and health clubs and the subsequent interest in bodybuilding are signs that masculinity is in a crisis. Men and masculinity have taken a beating over the last several decades. Between the women's movement, which has begun to inch men out of the power seat, and the men's movement, which drives men toward fraternal gatherings, masculinity seems to have been mislaid somewhere in the middle.

Masculinity is viewed as a sense of self-security, a reaffirmation of all the qualities that make a man a man, in his eyes and in the eyes of others. It is a desire to reestablish this lost sense of self-security that leads some men toward bodybuilding.[3] Modern men believe that a troubled sense of security can only be healed through a muscular body. Today, men have little other than their bodies to fall back on because our society is fixated on the notion that masculinity is determined primarily by outward appearance.

For centuries, men have been accorded the status of the stronger sex, while women have long been called the weaker sex. Our society continues, despite feminism, to give credence to this notion. Muscles have never figured into societal definitions or descriptions of femininity; women have never needed muscles to announce to the world that they are women. Yet to be a man without muscles is, for some, not to be a man at all.

Muscularity as masculinity is a bad idea for men because it places pressure on them to conform to a false sense of normalcy. It is an equally bad idea for women to accept because it creates a false ideal of typical male physical beauty, by perpetuating the myth and stereotype that a muscular man is the ultimate social or sexual mate.

Men react and identify with what they see outside of themselves more than with what they see inside themselves. Men are more likely to react to and identify with the types of men they see in their everyday activities than to the types of men they believe themselves to be. Men watch television, go to movies, read books, view pornography, or see advertisements that are very explicit in their respective representations of male physique and ideal masculinity. One would have to be dead not to notice these representations of male appearance. If an image is pounded into men's brains long enough, they will eventually see this image as a true depiction of what men ought to be.

Muscularity is perceived to be more than masculinity; it is also an indicator of sexual desire and perhaps a signal of sexual availability, a display of a male's search for a mate. This is not unlike the display of other male animals during their mating seasons. The peacock's display of his colorful tail feathers, for example, serves no purpose other than to attract a female partner.

There is no definitive or conclusive information available on how important male muscularity is to heterosexual women. Although surveys published in various periodicals provide some clues, they are not a fair and accurate source, since they represent only a percentage of a particular surveyed audience and not all women.

It is generally assumed in modern society that women are less concerned about men's muscles than they are about other male traits. Often we hear that women prefer men to be sensitive, nurturing, caring, and good fathers, rather than muscular. Muscles, perhaps as far as heterosexual women are concerned, are merely a bonus. Indeed, facial attractiveness may also rate higher with women than muscular bodies. Bodies lacking muscularity or definition can be hidden; unattractive faces cannot.

Why do some women think that male muscularity is important? Are women innately attracted to muscular men? Are women the female peacocks waiting for the right male to come along and fan out his tail of muscles? Are women being taught or told by a culture which emphasizes youth and beauty that muscularity is the ideal physical appearance of a male?

In the end, it may not matter what heterosexual women think about muscular men. What may be more important is that heterosexual men *believe* heterosexual women find male muscles important. *Muscle & Fitness* magazine tells us that men work out primarily to make themselves more attractive to women. Here, the emphasis on male bodybuilding is not health but being attractive to women. A buffed male body is "armor" worn in a "war" being fought among eligible bachelors looking for female partners.[4]

One reason for men to have muscular bodies is to save them from the "the shame" of being unmuscular.[5] Not only are the lack of muscles and an overweight body dead giveaways of being unmasculine, they are also shameful. It is not surprising that such sentiment appears in a magazine devoted exclusively to the world of bodybuilding. It would not benefit the magazine's subscription rate to print anything to the contrary. The magazine survives by shaming its readers into believing that having muscles or being a bodybuilder is what all men should strive to accomplish. If they do not, they are not men, or at the very least, they are undesirable men.

Why should men be ashamed of not having muscular bodies? What is society telling men who are skinny or fat? Basically, they are being told that they are unhealthy, unattractive, and undesirable. Even the perception of success is tied to muscular bodies.[6] Certainly, a hard body makes a man a successful weight lifter, but the author of this particular article seems to be attributing other kinds of success to having a hard body. Success is far too subjective a word and concept to be defined by the physical appearance of muscles. When most people think of success or of what makes them successful, it is highly unlikely that they turn to their bodies before turning to their bank accounts or investment portfolios.

SEX AND SALVATION

One area in which success and bodybuilding, or muscles, can pair is sex. A former Mr. USA titleholder believes that although men may say they lift weights for health reasons they also do it to make their bodies desirable. The former Mr. USA is absolutely right. With the exception of competitive bodybuilders, most men probably share Mr. USA's opinion. Following the age-old notion that all men are highly sexed, men are going to do whatever it takes to make themselves more desirable. Having a muscular body is believed to be the most effective, or the most successful, way of attracting sex partners. The hard body not only makes a man a desirable sex partner; it nearly guarantees successful and satisfying sex because the "chemistry" is right. If we believe this, "chemistry" is based strictly on physical appearance and nothing else.[7]

If sex is a physical act, and a human sexual response to another human is based first and foremost on the physical, a man with a well-built, muscular body is going to be noticed by a sexually interested onlooker long before a man with no noticeable muscles. There exists a survival-of-the-fittest attitude which suggests to us that only the strong and the buffed can pair "with the best." Here, "best" is equated with muscularity, and muscles become the preference of those interested in men as sexual mates.[8] Consequently, out-of-shape women and out-of-shape men are relegated to substandard sex lives and unsatisfying sexual experiences. The only thing that can save them is getting in shape so they can attract, and become, the right sex partner. Here is the "salvation" muscles can bring to a man. Muscles rescue the man from the sexless and lonely pit created by a skinny, flat, and unnatural body.[9]

The muscular male has become so stereotyped in our society as the ideal male that even male mannequins used in department and clothing stores are molded to fit the stereotype. *Muscle & Fitness* describes the current-day male mannequin as ". . . a strong, muscular hunk."[10] *People* magazine takes the ideal even further, by telling us about an artist in New York commissioned to design a male mannequin for a department store. The artist's ideal man stands "6′ 2″ with [a] 42″ chest, as opposed to the 6′-tall, 40″-chest industry standard."[11] Sam Fussell tells us that male mannequins are ones who "boast buzz-cuts and biceps."[12] Real-life men must strive to look like plastic dummies standing in store windows, if they are to be taken seriously as contenders for mating and sex.

Some even believe a muscular body can "save" a failing relationship.[13] Married couples who are having problems should forget the usual methods used to save a marriage and instead turn to bodybuilding because a hard body can put a failing marriage back on track. This notion is, of course, absurd because it ignores very real prob lems that married couples, or any two people in a relationship, face—problems that have nothing at all to do with muscles. It is conceivable that two people may very well be sexually compatible but at the same time emotionally destructive to each other and the relationship.

Hard bodies can increase sexual pleasure in ways that may or may not be true. The debate continues about whether sex is a physical act, a mental act, or both. Either way, we have been conditioned to believe that a muscular body is more sexually appealing. We have a physical reaction to a muscular body as much as we have a mental reaction to a muscular body. There is no proof, however, that such reactions are instinctual human reactions. What kind of reactions are they? Are they reactions experienced as a set of multiple reactions, or are they single reactions from one source? It would seem that our first reaction to anything, muscles included, is a visual one, and this may lead to both mental and physical reactions. When we see a muscular body, and this is what we are attracted to or interested in having sex with, we react both mentally and physically. Our mental reaction tells us that this is a person with whom we want to have sex. Our physical reaction is a feeling of lust. Although these reactions are very real, there is still no evidence they are instinctual human reactions uniform throughout the human race. These reactions must be considered culturally oriented and culturally created because in other cultures outside the West, muscles, or even physical appearance, play little or no part in mating or sexual affairs.

In his book *Little Big Men*, Alan Klein mentions the Jewish and Asian cultures as examples of other cultures that aspire to American ideals. Klein cites historian Paul Breines' examination of American Jewry and says that Breines "has examined the way in which Jews, traditionally perceived as nonphysical and weak, have reacted to the Holocaust by exaggerating hyper-masculine attributes and imitating their Nazi persecutors."[14] These attributes are, of course, muscle oriented, since "Nazi persecutors" were considered physically stronger than their Jewish prisoners. In this case, the attaining of a muscular build by Jewish men is used as an attempt to wipe away the ignominy of history, when Jewish men, as prisoners of the Nazis, were the weak being oppressed and murdered by the strong. In this instance, muscles have nothing to do with sex or being sexy. They are more a psychological advantage than anything else.

Asian men, according to Klein, "have been culturally perceived as non-physical. . . . Even martial arts expert Bruce Lee is perceived as being on the smallish side (that is, effeminate)."[15] Klein cites a situation in San Francisco, an area with a large Asian population, in which, according to an article in the *San Francisco Examiner*, increasing numbers of Asian women are having marital and sexual relationships with Caucasian men. Presumably, this is because Asian women are finding Caucasian men more appealing and attractive. In response to this, according to Klein, Asian men "have decided to present themselves visually as 'real men.'"[16] As previously mentioned, the Western standard of the real man is the muscled man. Asian men are certainly aware of this. A group of Asian men in San Francisco produced a calendar featuring Asian male bodybuilders in an effort to fight the stereotype depicting Asian men as being undesirable in Western culture.[17] Here is strong evidence that Western standards of sexiness are culturally produced and not innate in humans worldwide.

We are led to believe that muscular men can heighten sexual pleasure, that a muscular body somehow provides a sexual experience unmuscular bodies cannot. Muscles in men are seen mostly as sexual adornment worn to be more attractive, desirable, or sexy, to others, and an invitation to amorous or lustful onlookers. Such a notion is extremely presumptuous because it insinuates that all people are attracted to muscular bodies, which is not true.[18]

Because of society's preconceived idea that muscles equal sexiness, it is difficult for the unmuscular man not to feel inadequate and insecure about the physical appearance of his body. Muscular men are "privileged" to look as they do because it is they who will attract the better sex partners. Unmuscular men are forced to sit back and either be sexless or settle for solitary sex through masturbation, pornography, and fantasy.[19]

To feel good about themselves, to feel desirable, the unmuscular must rely on overstated recognition.[20] In other words, no one can feel wanted or beautiful without muscles unless they are being lied to by those who are wanted and beautiful. The danger in this is that such an overstated recognition places a relationship in peril because the relationship is then based on shallowness. Based on this we can only presume, then, that placing importance on muscular bodies and lauding such bodies as the ultimate sexual experience is not shallow behavior. This is not so according to one writer who claims that shallowness is the desire to have sex with only muscled sex partners. It is difficult to understand shallowness with two such disparate definitions of shallow behavior. It is particularly difficult when we also are told by this writer that women have the right to expect men to be physically attractive not only to women but to themselves as well. In fact, it is a man's "duty" to look good, since it is believed by some that women are only attracted to men who recognize their own attractiveness.[21]

It would seem, then, that muscles are the norm all men must strive to achieve if they are ever to have fulfilling sex and meaningful relationships. Then and only then will men be able to place themselves in a position to be highly desired by potential sex partners. *Muscle & Fitness* tells us that in naming the qualifications of what makes someone attractive physical appearance is near the top of the list.[22] *Muscle & Fitness* must believe this since they make the same argument two years later in a separate article and yet once again in 1995.[23]

MUSCLES EQUAL SURVIVAL

Muscle & Fitness maintains the belief that women especially prefer men with hard bodies over men with soft bodies. The publication claims that since women will in some ways compromise themselves for the sake of an attractive man[24]—and making the same claim two years later[25] and again in 1995[26]—then, accordingly, a muscular body is the best trait a man can possess and also the one quality to which a woman will find herself most attracted. These are also believed to be necessary to ensure survival of the family.[27] Once again, *Muscle & Fitness* takes a theme and runs with it, using the same argument in the August 1995 issue.[28]

To regard muscularity as an attractive quality because it is a representation of survival of the family is antiquated thinking that has no place in the modern world. *Muscle & Fitness* seems to disagree, painting a picture of the twentieth-century muscular man dragging his mate by the hair into his two-bedroom, two-bath condo.

Joe Weider, publisher of *Muscle & Fitness* and head of his own bodybuilding empire, argues that a muscular body is something separate and apart from the other elements of desirability. Once again, muscles are placed on a list of "desirable qualities," leaving the unmuscular man short of an essential attribute for inspiring desire.[29]

Although Weider does not seem to consider muscularity a necessary requirement for modern man's survival, he does attempt to convince us that our reactions to muscles are "instinctive and learned responses."[30] What is unfair here is Weider's coupling of the instinctive with the learned, two very different areas of human or animal makeup.

One of our most basic instincts is to eat, but as children, we must be taught what to eat and how to obtain what we eat. This is no different from, for example, a lion cub who knows instinctively that it wants to eat meat but must learn from its mother how to kill. Instinct does not tell a lion cub *how* to kill, only that killing is what it must do to survive. Likewise, humans instinctively want to have sex and, depending upon orientation, will gravitate toward an appropriate gender—male, female, or both. Human instinct, however, does not guide us toward what type of man or woman with whom we want to have sex. This we must learn.

The thought processes we have encountered and subsequently learned throughout our lives have taught us that muscular men make ideal sex partners. Such arenas of culture in our society as advertising, film, and television have been our teachers. Propaganda spit out from cultural money machines has brainwashed the majority of us into believing that ultimate sex is not possible without ultimate sex partners. This is the same money machinery that for years has promoted notions that women must live up to certain standards of physical beauty to be considered sexually desirable. The only difference is that now it is considered wrong or taboo or passé to objectify women (though this is still done), but it is not considered wrong to do the same to men. The play is the same. Only the players have changed.

Desiring certain sexual types cannot be considered instinct in humans because not all of us are attracted to the same type of sexual partners. Our *desire* for sex is collectively instinctual, but this is where the similarity ends. Weider's argument, however, does not take into consideration the processes and results of human evolution, nor does it allow for the possibility that as humans evolve physically and socially over time so too will instinctual and learned processes. Modern society demands we use our instinct and learning in much different ways than in the past.[31]

As our environment changes so too does our reaction to elements within our environment. Evolutionary change in human perception must be accounted for. If it is not, how can we explain the ever-changing cultural aspects of our society? There have been major shifts throughout history in, for example, our perception of female beauty, or even of beauty in general. For example, what Reubens saw in his art as his contemporary female beauty is not considered beautiful in today's world.

Without shifting perceptions of human behavior, our society would never have seen the numerous social movements that have dominated certain historical eras. Change in perceptions greatly contributed to, for example, the suffragist movement, the Civil Rights movement, the women's movement, the environmental movement, and the gay rights movement. None of these would have come about had it not been for changing perceptions of women, blacks, the environment, or gays. None of these movements can continue without continuing change in the associated perceptions of these groups.

Weider disagrees, saying that little has changed in the reactions men have to beautiful women. He makes the assumption that images of attractive women during primeval times are consistent with twentieth-century definitions of female attractiveness. Furthermore, he assumes that unattractive women are not worthy of responses from muscular men who cannot look beyond their own acquired attractiveness.[32]

Weider does not limit his beliefs to men's responses to women. He further claims that throughout the ages women have always responded positively to a muscular male body.[33] Once again, Weider is assuming that such a response to a muscular male is instinctual and unchanging and that such a reaction to the muscular male represents the reaction of *all* heterosexual women. He does not allow room for some women's belief that muscular men—particularly those men who are at a competitive bodybuilding level—appear "freakish" and not at all attractive. Furthermore, he does not recognize that there are some men who share this opinion.[34] What Weider emphasizes is his belief that muscular bodies are a part of age-old mating rituals that are somehow primeval in nature.[35]

Weider's beliefs clearly stem from his position as head of a bodybuilding empire. Such beliefs are necessary for the world of bodybuilding and physical fitness to continue as a money-making business venture. To believe otherwise would do his credibility and his bank account no good at all.

MUSCLE MEDICINE

Despite the overwhelming belief that a muscular body equals a healthy body, muscular men are not immune to viruses and diseases which cause ill health. Having muscles will not save anyone who suffers from a life-threatening illness any more than it will save a failing marriage or relationship. *Muscle & Fitness* magazine wants us to believe that weight lifting will decrease the rate of human aging, increase strength, keep fatal diseases at bay, and give a man's muscles a youthful appearance.[36] All of this is good advertising for the bodybuilding and fitness industries, but it is incomplete, misleading, and potentially dangerous medical advice for men.

The fact that exercise and bodybuilding increase your strength and endurance is a given. A youthful appearance can only be construed to mean having the muscles of a young boy and is not so much a physical advantage as it is a psychological one—a way for a man who is growing old to hang on to his youth and the fading image of his masculinity. A youthful appearance is as much a desired and glorified quality in men as physical beauty and pronounced muscularity. Youth is a man's "dominant dream" because a well-muscled body is "that picture of eternal adolescence."[37]

Youth as beauty is a means of escape that many use to ignore the inevitable onset of old age. After all, our culture reviles the elderly more than it reveres them. Looking young, whether by having a muscular body or by any other means, has a greater effect on our minds than it does our bodies. We think that in looking younger we will feel better about ourselves. This may be true, but it is more of a response to societal beliefs than to individual beliefs. There is nothing wrong with feeling or being young, or even feeling or being beautiful or muscular for that matter. There *is* something wrong with putting so much emphasis on youth and beauty that it makes the elderly feel inadequate and out of place.

Exercise maintains a healthy body. The American College of Sports Medicine's position is that "strength training of a moderate intensity, sufficient to develop and maintain fat-free weight, should be an integral part of an adult fitness program."[38] This position includes weight training as a *part* of an overall fitness program. To highlight bodybuilding in particular, without including the multitude of other exercises that are just as beneficial to the body (if not better for it), is an attempt by the bodybuilding and weight-lifting industries to establish muscle building as the premiere form of exercise and the ultimate path to staying healthy and attractive, thereby exploiting a growing loss of male self-esteem and manhood in those who have unmuscular bodies.

*   *   *

Most men do not have bodybuilder's bodies, and a large percentage of men probably do not want them. To place muscular bodies in the realm of idealized perfection is elitist and exclusionary, not to mention psychologically and socially damaging to the men and women who do not have such bodies.

The onus of responsibility is on the unmuscular who must live up to the muscular's standard of beauty and desirability. It is the unmuscular who must make changes in appearance to reach the level of supremacy that is the privilege of the muscular. No consideration is given to the fact that bodybuilders and the muscular should change *their* opinions and outlooks and align themselves to the way of thinking of the vast majority of their unmuscular counterparts.

One reason for such diversity between the muscular and the unmuscular is that bodybuilders often believe that being muscular is a *natural* appearance. *Muscle & Fitness* magazine tells us that the physical results of bodybuilding will make people *believe* you were born with a pumped-up body, that it is natural.[39] Yet Sam Fussell says that "a natural bodybuilder is an oxymoron. . . . There's nothing natural about it."[40]

No man is born with a muscular body, at least not in the way muscularity is currently defined. Some men have natural definition in their bodies without doing a bit of physical exercise. However, these natural beauties cannot measure up to, or compete with, these predetermined standards of acceptable muscularity. Furthermore, let any clothed man tell a prospective muscle-minded sexual partner that his build is naturally well-defined, and he probably will not be having sex with anyone but himself.

Like it or not, muscles on men represent sex. It doesn't matter whether heterosexual women believe this because heterosexual women did not create the equation. Heterosexual women are only expected to abide by the solution. That is, if heterosexual women want to have the ultimate sexual experience, they had better find themselves in bed with muscular men. They also had better be in shape themselves. Otherwise, none of us can be satisfied.

Chapter 11

Is He Cute? Gay Male Culture

Although the majority of gay men are quick to protest the mainstream stereotypes of gay men, they are often slow in challenging the projected stereotypes gay male culture imposes upon its own society. Raymond M. Berger, author of *Gay and Gray*, writes, "Preoccupation with potential discrimination by outsiders often obscures actual discrimination within a minority group's own ranks."[1]

The majority of these stereotypes have been created and perpetuated by mainstream society and nearly always are attacked by gay men for projecting an atypical image of a gay man's appearance, occupation, or lifestyle. Although some gay men expend inordinate amounts of time and energy attempting to dispel mainstream society's stereotypes of gay men, these same men fail to acknowledge their part in perpetuating the very same stereotypes within their own culture. The difference is that when heterosexuals stereotype gays it is called oppression or homophobia, but when gay men stereotype gay men, it is considered a celebration and recognition of an alternate lifestyle. This creates a double standard, although few within gay male culture seem willing to acknowledge it as such.

In cities across the country where homosexuality has become more and more visible, annual gay pride or gay freedom events are held to celebrate the diversity and the existence of gay culture. In larger cities—Los Angeles, San Francisco, New York—parades become the focal point of the day's festivities. The contingents in these parades are partially, if not predominantly, made up of the very stereotypes of gay men perpetuated by mainstream society and reviled by the gay community.

A contingent of drag queens in a gay pride or gay freedom parade is met with applause and whistles by gay onlookers. The same is true when a flatbed truck loaded with men dressed in leather passes by. Yet when news of the event—an event often covered by major mainstream newspapers and television networks—is spread across America, gay men attack and blame the media for exploiting the myth that all gay men are drag queens who harbor a desire to be women or men who are obsessed with mysterious sexual practices. Some gays avoid responsibility for the changing of gay stereotypes by saying they cannot control the mainstream media. Yet they fail to realize that they have complete control over what the media sees. If gay people are blind to their own lack of responsibility to dispel the myths imposed by straight society, can they be any more clear-sighted when it comes to the creation and perpetuation of stereotypes within their own community?

Gay men are attracted to men who are beautiful in much the same way as straight men are attracted to beautiful women. Men are socialized to believe that beauty is necessary for sexual and emotional satisfaction. Young boys are socialized by their parents' and other adult relatives' ideas, television programs and commercials, films, popular music, teen magazines, and their peers. Since all gay men were at one time boys, who probably struggled with their homosexual identification at a young age, they more than likely absorbed society's dogma about what does and what does not constitute female beauty. As these boys matured into gay men, they used what they had been taught to believe is the ideal woman to seek and identify the ideal man.

Although gay men have created their own problems with regard to male beauty within their own culture, they, as men, still play a role in defining female beauty. Because gay men were conditioned or socialized to grow up to be straight men, they cannot forget what they have learned in terms of what is and what is not considered female beauty. As adults, and despite their attraction to men, gay men help perpetuate the myths of female beauty. Even without looking at women as potential sex partners or mates, gay men continue to place women in categories of beautiful and ugly. For example, notice how some gay men are almost obsessed with female beauty pageants and female celebrities.

Women and gay men have much in common in their efforts to dispel popular myths of beauty and physical perfection. Within the boundaries of their respective battlefields, women and gay men share the distinction of being sex objects, exploited to the extent that if they fail to meet the accepted criteria of being beautiful they are worth nothing more than a passing, pitiful glance or a ridicule-filled laugh. Whereas the exploitation of women as sex objects and the subsequent ideals of beauty come from the opposite sex, it is other gay men who create an arena for the objectification of gay men and a definition of gay male beauty.

Beauty in gay male culture, as it is espoused and portrayed by those who make up that culture, is not so much a stereotype as it is an archetype. The male form, as long as it boasts a beautiful face and a muscular body, is the maypole around which gay men celebrate and worship their sexuality.

Whether it is real or fantasy, the goal of many gay men is to fall in love with a good-looking man. If any gay man were asked to list the attributes of what he looks for when pursuing a mate, physical appearance will at some point show up on the list. Appearance may not be at the head of all gay men's lists, although it will certainly be number one on many of them, but it will eventually surface somewhere. Often physical appearance is an afterthought: "I want a man who is kind, generous, stable, and mature. Oh, and it wouldn't hurt if he is gorgeous, too." This type of statement, which is not uncommon among gay men, implies a gay man's willingness to *settle* for an unattractive man if that is all he can find, but a beautiful man is the dominant preference.

Physical attraction and dating are precursors to falling in love. Of the two, physical attraction is the starting point at which gay men begin to follow their ideals of male beauty—ideals of beauty universally accepted and defined by gay male culture itself. Gay men, similar to straight women, have lost the ability to determine their own ideas of beauty and whom they are, or can be, attracted to because they allow themselves to base their personal opinions on cultural interpretations rather than on their own individual interpretations.

A gay man's search for beauty is unending. He may find himself attracted to another man but may never approach that man because the next man he sees may be more attractive, and the next even more attractive, and so on. There is always the chance that the next man who comes through the door or around the corner is going to be better looking.

Often, when a gay man finds himself attracted to another man, he cannot initiate a meeting until he verifies the other man's attractiveness. Usually such a verification is made by asking a friend, "Do you think he's cute?" Why do gay men seek the opinions of other gay men to qualify beauty? One reason may be for the sake of reputation. Gay men like to be visible to other gay men. If a gay man is seen on the arm of a beautiful man, his ego is stroked and he is envied by friends and strangers alike.

In the eyes of many in the heterosexual world, and to a large extent those in the homosexual world, gay men live their lives with two purposes in mind—to have sex and to have it frequently. Over past decades, many explanations have been offered to determine gay men's seemingly insatiable appetite for sex. One common explanation for gay men's abundant sexual desires is that they spent so many years suppressing their true sexual needs—to have sex with men and not women—that when they finally came to accept their homosexuality they looked for and found multiple sex partners to make up for lost time.

Another popular explanation is that since gay men are men they must live up to society's standards and expectations of male or masculine behavior. In the introduction to *Gay Men: The Sociology of Male Homosexuality*, Martin P. Levine writes:

> What makes gay men so sexually active? Rejecting past psychoanalytic explanations, most experts consider male gender role as the primary cause: men in our society are told it is masculine to have numerous sexual relations as well as sex divorced from emotional commitment; gays are socialized as men during most of their formative years; accordingly, their sexual behavior reflects obedience to masculinity's dictates.[2]

In more recent times, however, explanations of gay men and sex have taken on a more political tone. Sexual freedom and promiscuity are means by which gay men act out against oppression. Activist and author Larry Kramer says, "The concept of making a virtue out of sexual freedom, e.g., promiscuity, . . . came about because gay men had nothing to call their own but their sexuality."[3]

However, not everyone places the responsibility for gay men's sexual freedom on heterosexual oppression of gays. In the gay news magazine *Frontiers,* Michael Nava writes, "Heterosexual culture tells us that homosexuality is about sex, and nothing else; much of the gay subculture not only sends the same message but congratulates itself on its liberated views."[4] Once again, we find a double standard at work.

It is sometimes difficult to make a distinction between sex and beauty in gay male culture because the two are so often and so closely linked. This is not to say that only beautiful gay men are having sex; it is just that the archetype of gay male beauty represents the ideal sex partner and the ideal sexual experience, that is, "the young, white mesomorph."[5] This is only partially true, and it is an incomplete picture of the physical types of gay men who are desired sex partners.

To be young is not enough. Certainly there was a time in gay male culture when being young was enough to qualify a gay man as being beautiful. As a fifty-year-old gay man explains in *The Arena of Masculinity,* "The business that one could make over one's body into the images that one desired, it was never true before the seventies. People who looked good in gay bars looked good because they were young and they had that kind of body 'naturally.'"[6] This is no longer the case. In today's gay male culture, youth does not automatically equal beauty but instead has become one item on a long list of qualifiers.

Growing old in gay culture has long been equated with growing ugly. Although the belief or myth that a man in straight culture becomes better looking as he grows older by becoming a *silver fox,* the same belief or myth does not exist in gay male culture. Older gay men are often ostracized from the gay community and are sometimes unwelcome, or not fully represented, in social, professional, and political activities that make up the day-to-day existence of younger gay men. For example, older gay men infrequently visit gay bars, popular among younger gay men, because older gay men are often treated as an intrusion.[7]

Also, black men and men of other racial and ethnic minorities are grossly underrepresented in cultural definitions and descriptions of gay male beauty. The white male is by far the prevailing example of the ideal gay male sex partner. This skirting of the line of racism, disguised and couched in terms of personal taste, is surprising because gay male culture is a community that prides itself on diversity and claims to set an example for the rest of the world in racial and sexual tolerance. For such claims, the gay community is incredibly lax in promoting the existence of men of color in its media and other tools of communication.

THE REAL MEN OF GAY SEX

The preponderant presence of the beautiful, young, and white male as the ultimate sex partner in gay male culture is clearly evidenced by taking even a scant look at gay male pornography. Nowhere are male beauty, physical appearance, youth, and whiteness more glorified than in this aspect of gay male culture. Pornography also offers gay men yet another opportunity to discover and learn about masculinity. After all, "[i]t is not irrelevant that the new gay image of virility is most often illustrated in pornography."[8]

Pornography is a conduit through which sexual desire is channeled when real-life sexual outlets are not available or desired. Because the types of men used in gay male pornography are so exhaustively one-sided, the argument can be made that a gay man's search for real-life sexual activity is heavily prejudiced by what he sees on videotapes or in magazines.

It is commonly argued that heterosexual pornography plays a major part in male violence against women and also straight men's expectations of how their female sex partners should look (e.g., large breasts, shaved vaginas). If this is true, cannot the same argument be made for gay male imagery in gay male pornography? Is it possible for a gay man who watches gay male pornography of two, or more (as is often the case), white, beautiful, and physically perfect men having sex *not* to expect his own real-life sexual partners to duplicate the video images?

The pornography business is said to be a 7-billion-dollar industry.[9] Although the majority of this industry is aimed at heterosexual men, a fair share is claimed by pornography aimed at gay men. A conservative guess at the number of pornographic videos aimed at gay men would be 10,000 titles. Walking into the gay male pornography section of a video store is like entering a restaurant. Men can choose from a menu the type of pornography or type of man in which they are interested. Selections vary from "Men of Color" (always a comparatively small section and, by virtue of its separation from other titles, an implication that men of color are merely a personal taste of the white gay male majority and not a viable contender for icon status) to "Hunks" to "Bondage and Spanking."

The number of pornographic videos rented by gay men has never been publicized.[10] Rental activity must be high, particularly since in the so-called gay ghettos (i.e., San Francisco, Los Angeles, New York City) the combined number of establishments renting or showing gay male pornography is well in the hundreds.

Consequently, it is impossible to dismiss how images of men and male physical appearance in pornography affect gay men's ability to self-define male beauty and gay male sex. Gay male pornography teaches gay men how to be sexual not only in sexual practices but also in sexual selection. In *The Beauty Myth,* Naomi Wolf suggests that human sexual urge is something learned, not something that is instinctual.[11] Although Wolf's statements were written in regard to women, female images, and sexual behavior as they relate to heterosexual pornography, the statements are no less true for gay men, gay male images, and gay male sexual behavior in gay pornography.

What exactly are gay men learning from watching gay male pornography? They are not learning how to *have* sex but rather what type of men with whom they should be having sex and also what gay men must do to their bodies to be considered sexy. In addition, gay men are learning with whom they should *not* have sex and also what male physical types could never be considered sexy.

Men are cast in gay male pornographic films to fill one of two roles—to play a character who has sex or to play a supporting, nonsexual role. The former is an archetype, the latter a stereotype.

The stereotyped role is one the story needs to form a bridge between the men who are going to have sex and the sex scenes themselves. Often these characters are schoolteachers, prison wardens, video store cashiers, or drag queens hosting a party. Their function is twofold: they serve as a means of introducing two of the men who will have sex, and they provide a bit of comic relief in the story line. Their role, and even their presence in the film, is irrelevant. Most men watching gay pornography pay little attention to these characters and probably fast-forward to the sex scenes. The men playing these nonsex roles are usually older, obese, thin, effeminate, or any combination of these characteristics. In other words, they are not desired sex partners. They are rarely, if ever, seen having sex in a gay pornographic film. The producers and directors of these films know that few, if any, gay men want to sit and watch older, obese, thin, or effeminate men engaged in sexual activity.

The men in gay pornography who are actually allowed to have sex are quite different from those men playing the prison wardens and schoolteachers. These men are the archetypes of gay male beauty. They are the gods, in all their physical and naked glory. As gay men watch these videos, what seeps into their minds is the message that to have ultimate gay male sexual experiences they must first find and then be accepted by men who meet the rigid standards of beauty established in pornography. The message is a simple and clear one: By having sexual experiences with men who are less than perfect, gay men are having sexual experiences that are also less than perfect.

Sometime in the course of evolution of gay male pornography, body hair became passé, and men with body hair all but disappeared from such videos. It is difficult to pinpoint the origins of gay male body shaving. Perhaps it was an idea lifted from the world of competitive bodybuilding, since contestants shave their body hair to better display their muscles. Or, as others have theorized, the removal of body hair may have come about in response to the AIDS crisis. Some equate body hair with sexual experience and further equate that experience with AIDS.[12]

Whenever, wherever, or why body-hair shaving began, it, similar to muscular bodies, quickly became a standard casting criterion in gay male pornography and soon a must in gay male culture if gay men were to fit within accepted norms of male attractiveness. As Richard D. Mohr notes in *Gay Ideas*, "Hairiness is dropped from gay male porn, for while it is naturally male, it socially connotes age, and the typical consumer of porn does not want age in his fantasies unless he is specifically looking for a daddy or bear type."[13] That being hairy makes one seem old is but one of the many messages gay men receive from pornography.

Gay male actors in pornographic films began this phenomenon by shaving the pubic hair from their testicles and trimming back, or sometimes shaving off completely, the pubic hair above the penis. As it turns out, the removal of the pubic hair makes the genitals look larger, and therefore more appealing, to the pornographic audience and consumer. The bigger-is-better mentality is not reserved solely for women's breasts. A gay man wanting to be cast in a pornographic film stands little chance if his penis is not, at the very least, above average in size, an average often inflated in the minds of gay men.

Because the anus plays such a large role in gay male sex, the hair around the opening and in between the buttocks is also removed. This ritual is not so different from women in straight pornography who have shaved vaginas. Although body hair is natural on both men and women, it prevents an unobstructed view of the opening—the vagina or male anus—being penetrated by a penis or licked by a tongue. As the camera zooms in for a close-up, the actors cease to be human beings and instead become only hairless male sex organs and body orifices.

What results from the purposeful removal of body hair is that in the real world hairy genitals and anuses, along with excessive or unshaped chest hair and hair on the back, have become taboo or, even worse, not sexy. Advertisements for body hair removal appear frequently in gay-oriented publications.[14]

Pornography is entrenched in gay male culture, as are the male archetypes and stereotypes it creates. Pornography goes beyond simply creating icons of male beauty and ideal sex partners; it trivializes gay males in ways that make gay men playthings instead of human beings.

Gay male pornography is not only film footage of men having oral or anal sex; it is also videotaped acts of bondage, sadomasochism, spanking, and even rape. In his book *The Culture of Desire,* Frank Browning writes, "A few minutes into almost any gay leather porn flick, one encounters the macho dudes who 'beat' their boys into submission, slapping them hard across the jaw and the ass, yanking a mouth to a mock-macho crotch, as the yanked-on one moans, 'Yeah, Daddy, yeah!'"[15] In many of these videos, men who sometimes look more like young boys than mature adults are forced into submissive, helpless situations, such as being tied facedown on a bed or hammock with their legs spread wide apart, while a group of stronger men, often dressed in leather and carrying whips or riding crops, stand in a circle and masturbate. Eventually, the submissive man is penetrated with a large artificial penis or a man's fist and lower arm. Next, the men standing in the circle each take their turn at having intercourse with the man who is tied down. When the camera shows the submissive man's face, it is difficult to determine if his expression is one of excitement and pleasure or one of fear and pain.

Although video may be the primary means by which images of sexual partners are projected onto gay male culture, hard-core and soft-core pornographic magazines also contribute to the ideology of gay male sex and beauty. Hard-core magazines generally contain still photographs of scenes from video pornography and differ only in that the men are frozen as inanimate objects of sexual fantasy. Soft-core gay male magazines are filled with photographs of men posing for the camera in various stages of undress and arousal. Although these magazines may be less blatant in sexual imagery, they duplicate the efforts of hard-core magazines and video in creating the ideal sexual partner by utilizing the same archetypes of gay male appearance.

In addition to fueling sexual fantasies, magazines provide gay men with the opportunity to purchase various items that enhance sexual pleasure or the ability to attract a more favorable sex partner. One of the most common items available to gay men is a vacuum pump that is used to temporarily enlarge the penis, a gadget which merely exploits the stereotype that men with large penises are more sexually desirable than men with small penises. Text for these advertisements furthers this exploitation by telling the consumer to "take the big plunge and pump your way to bigger, harder, more powerful pleasures." Other ad copy asks, "Have you ever envied men who had tremendous penis dimensions, erect measurements of 8, 9, or even 10 inches?" Pitied is the man whose erection measures less than eight inches.

In the age of AIDS and safe sex, telephone sex has become a thriving industry. In gay male magazines and newspapers across the country, telephone sex is advertised with phenomenal frequency. Similar to its predecessors, magazines and videos, telephone sex is yet another area of gay male culture in which male archetypes of sexual desire and beauty are used to instill the notion that men who have pretty faces and muscular bodies are every gay man's sexual fantasy.

One advertisement for a twenty-four-hour fantasy service phone line pictures three men: one wears a jock strap, the other, a pair of bikini underwear, and the third, a leather thong. All of them are attractive and have bodies resembling Greek statues. Above the photograph are the words, "Head Quarters. Where Fantasies Come Alive!" In another advertisement, an attractive, well-built man wearing a jock strap, leans against a wall and holds a phone receiver to his ear while his other hand cups the bulge of his penis. "Fantasy Men" is printed in large red letters above the photograph.

How can gay men escape the suggestion that fantasy equals attractive, well-built men? What about the gay man who does not look like the men in these telephone sex advertisements? How must he feel about himself when, in essence, he is being told that he is undesirable and unattractive, that he is no gay man's fantasy?

GOING FOR THE GAY DOLLAR

Male archetypes in gay male culture are not limited only to pornography and the telephone sex industry. Beautiful and well-built men are the mainstays of advertisers wishing to claim their share of gay men's money. There is no better way for advertisers to catch the eye of gay male consumers, no matter what the product, than to use idealized male bodies in their advertisements. A look through most any magazine or periodical aimed at gay men reveals the extent to which a preconceived or predefined idea of male beauty dominates gay male culture. In many cases, the men used in advertisements have absolutely nothing to do with the product or service being offered for sale. It is often difficult to determine what, exactly, is being sold—the product/service or the men as fantasy sex objects. The following are some examples.

An advertisement for a framing store uses two shirtless men to advertise a 50 percent off sale. Maybe the connection here is that the men are 50 percent naked.

A restaurant advertisement features a photograph of a shirtless man with rippling stomach muscles. Unless a consumer lives in the city in which the restaurant is located, they would not even know that the ad is for an eating establishment; the words food or restaurant are never used in the advertisement.

A Southern California resort hotel for gay men uses a photograph of a man's torso. Printed alongside the photograph is a blurb of information about the hotel that ends with, "Offering all the amenities you deserve." Because any gay man reading or seeing this advertisement is already influenced by a cultural belief that the man in the photo represents ideal beauty, he is naturally going to wonder if the man is one of the amenities being offered.

In an advertisement for a travel agency, a silhouette of a naked man appears. The photograph is captioned, "America's best looking young men are waiting to be your servants in first class surroundings all the way."

An ad for a mortgage company uses a photograph of a man sleeping in his underwear. "Dreams do come true!" the copy reads.

A photograph of a naked man accompanies an ad for a viatical company that is clearly aimed at men who are HIV positive or who have AIDS. Similarly targeted ads for nutritional products regularly feature attractive models. All of this seems to indicate that only beautiful gay men contract or have AIDS. Consequently, the Los Angeles Gay and Lesbian Community Services Center created its own ad campaign to remind us that AIDS does not discriminate. Their ads featured models showing the physically altering effects of AIDS, similar to ads placed by clothing manufacturer Benetton, which used men near death and an image of then-President Reagan covered with lesions. Others are not so willing. As the founder of *POZ*, a magazine marketed to the AIDS community, says, "[L]ike any magazine, we try to make everyone in *POZ* as attractive as possible."[16] This is important to *POZ* because the magazine's survival depends on advertising revenue.

Advertisers of hotels, restaurants, cruise lines, medical centers, and the like have a keen sense for extolling the perfect gay male image in an effort to entice—and arouse—customers. Similarly, clothing manufacturers and their advertisements have made apparel one of the most important assets gay men can possess—as long as the men have faces and bodies that complement or justify their right and privilege to wear the outfits being advertised.

Not all gay men are prone to watching pornography and are therefore not influenced by this industry's projected ideals of gay male beauty and physical appearance. However, all gay men do buy clothing, and, more than likely, at some point in their lives, they are exposed to clothing advertisements, which have become (or perhaps always have been) a kind of pornography in their own right.

The men used in clothing advertisements differ from the men in pornography only in that they are clothed—if a man can be considered clothed while wearing only a jock strap or a pair of mesh underwear—and are not photographed in overtly sexual situations. Whether a model advertising clothing is wearing next to nothing or is fully dressed in a tuxedo, the imagery of physical appearance and male beauty are the same—Herculean bodies and faces to die for. Since one end result of pornography is the glorification of the perfect sex partner, clothing advertisements celebrate the notion that without the proper attire, and the perfect body to complement that attire, a gay man is invisible and will spend his days and nights wanting sex but never having it.

A catalog specifically created to advertise clothing to gay men is described on the cover as "The Catalog for the Gay Man." On the first page, the creators proclaim that the catalog "openly recognizes and reveres gay style." In effect, and with only a few words, this statement singlehandedly reduces the image of gay male beauty and style to a thirty-five-page advertisement.

THE GAY MEDIA

Editors and publishers of gay male magazines are no less knowledgeable than advertisers when it comes to the success generated by the use of the male body as a selling tool. With tremendous regularity, gay male periodicals fill their covers or front pages with beautiful men to attract readers. Some of the more long-lasting publications do not have to resort to this tactic because they succeed on name recognition or reputation. Others, particularly newer publications desperate for their share of readers, do not have this luxury. Still, the long-lasting ones will at times use naked, beautiful men to push a particular issue or story.

It is sometimes difficult to make a correlation between the naked, beautiful man and the accompanying article. In most cases, it is impossible to determine what one has to do with the other. In an issue of *Christopher Street,* the cover story is on David Kopay, a professional football player who, in 1977, publicly revealed his homosexuality. The cover photograph is of Kopay wearing only a towel, showing the readers he is still in good physical shape. The article is accompanied by two photographs in which Kopay is completely naked.

In the first photograph, his genitals are in shadows, while in the second they are fully lit. Was Kopay photographed in the nude simply because the article appeared in a magazine aimed at gay men? It is highly unlikely that Kopay would have been photographed in the nude had this same article appeared in *Sports Illustrated, Time,* or *Newsweek.* Why then should he appear naked in a gay magazine? It is because he is considered good-looking and sexy, and he, or rather his body, guarantees sales.[17]

In another example, *Genre* magazine's Fall 1991 cover story, "Battered Husbands: Domestic Violence in Gay Relationships," features a cover photograph of a man who is presumably naked (the lighting used in the photograph makes it difficult to determine the extent of the model's dress) and posed in a way that suggests he is cowering from a would-be attacker. The photographs used to illustrate the article are of men in their underwear who are presented more as sexual fantasies than as victims of abuse or the abuser. Although both men appear wearing only a pair of underwear, one of the men is photographed from behind to draw attention to his well-shaped buttocks. As if this were not sexually suggestive enough in itself, the underwear is drawn up between the buttocks and immediately brings the reader's attention to the man or rather the buttocks and the sex they represent. The text and substance of domestic violence in gay male relationships becomes secondary.[18]

The *Frontiers* article cited earlier is another example. The article, which intellectualizes on the sexualization of homosexuality and societal definitions of masculinity, is illustrated with several photographs of two men wrestling. The symbolism created by wrestling is clever, but undoubtedly, this particular sport was chosen to illustrate this article because wrestling is homoerotic. Wrestling is frequently used in gay male pornography as a prelude to, or a substitute for, sex.

Photographs of two men boxing could have been used and the same point of man against man would have been made. However, boxing is more brutal than it is homoerotic. Physical contact in boxing is limited to fists landing against an opponent's torso and face and would have been more appropriate, certainly more symbolic, as an illustration for *Genre* magazine's article on domestic violence. Wrestling, on the other hand, is a full-contact sport and has overtones of aggressive sex, particularly when the wrestlers' positions are frozen in a photograph. The pleasant looks on the models' faces in the *Frontiers* photographs indicate sexual satisfaction more than a determination to win the wrestling match.[19]

Using photographs of naked men, or ones that are sexually suggestive, to accompany articles on serious subjects is a ploy used by editors and publishers to attract the attention and money of gay men. Such a tactic is an insult to a gay male reader's intelligence. The implication is that a gay man's mind cannot be stimulated without first stimulating his libido.

Editors and publishers of gay male periodicals, similar to advertisers and pornography producers, know that sex sells, and they exploit the ideals of gay male beauty and physical appearance accordingly. Gay periodicals, such as *Frontiers*, *Christopher Street*, and *Genre*, are not blatantly or admittedly published as erotica, even though this is to some extent exactly what they are. *Frontiers* stands out as a prime example. With few exceptions, the cover of each issue of *Frontiers* is graced with a near-naked, white, well-built male model. In some issues, the magazine includes a centerfold, always a man with a muscular body. *Frontiers* labels itself as a news magazine for the gay community. The inclusion of a centerfold solely for purposes of sexual stimulation, however, turns the magazine into pornography. A similar centerfold in *Time* or *Newsweek* would be ridiculous and would never be allowed by its editors and publishers or by the public. Yet in *Frontiers*, a gay news magazine, a centerfold is considered appropriate, even mandatory.

It is nearly impossible for gay men to look through these periodicals and not become sexually aroused. Moreover, the power possessed by these publications lies in the physical images they project onto gay male culture (as well as straight culture). In *The Culture of Desire,* we read, "[Gay periodicals] are, or claim to be, 'whole life' papers that tell gay, mostly urban, male readers what it means to be gay in America."[20] As a result, gay men are unwittingly positioned to be very particular when searching for a partner; they are no longer able to rely on personal, individual tastes and desires unprejudiced by external factors.

* * *

Beauty, like ugliness, is natural, as long as it remains an individual's interpretation of what is natural. Beauty ceases to be natural when its definition is dependent upon, and then glorified by, a group or society as a whole. Attractiveness is desired and desirable; unattractiveness is rejected and repulsive. When beauty becomes paramount in a culture or society, it becomes a tool of discrimination and a reason for segregation.

Attractive gay men do discriminate against unattractive gay men. Consider the popular private sex parties that are commonly found in cities housing large gay male communities. These parties often restrict entrance to those gay men who live up to current standards of male beauty. Invitations are offered only to men who are considered physically attractive and sexually desirable by other gay men. An organizer of safe-sex parties in Los Angeles publicly and proudly admits that he discriminates, regarding entrance to his parties, based on looks.[21]

Because of these attitudes, some members of the gay community promote attractiveness as an enviable asset, in much the same way as Hitler promoted the Aryan race as being pure, the Ku Klux Klan promotes white supremacy or some heterosexuals promote their superiority over homosexuals. Although these comparisons may be dramatic and far-reaching, they are nonetheless accurate. If they were not, the popular and dominant aspects of gay male culture, such as the pornography, advertising, and telephone sex industries, would not rely so heavily on accepted images of gay male beauty to promote and sell their services or products. Propaganda is propaganda. It does not matter whether it comes from a Nazi leader espousing ethnic superiority to a nation or from a handful of pornography producers, advertisers, hosts of safe-sex parties, and editors espousing physical superiority to a community.

To take away the beauty propaganda that is consistently forced upon gay men would drastically alter the texture of gay male culture. This culture would cease to exist as it currently does in its representation of a gay male lifestyle.

It is not likely, however, that this change will occur. As it is in straight culture, the onus of change is placed upon the shoulders of unattractive or unmuscular gay men. It is this group, clearly the majority, who are expected to live up to the expectations and standards imposed by the minority. The muscular are not about to give up what separates them from the rest of the crowd. Who among them would want to let go of a godlike status? And sadly, who among the mortals would want them to?

It is no wonder, then, that a New York gym would use "No Pecs, No Sex" as its advertising slogan.[22]

Chapter 12

Where Do We Go from Here?

Where will this phenomenon of male beauty go? Where will this public exposition and disposition of an idealized male body type end?

If in the works of artists and writers there once existed an idealized and stereotyped image of the male body, and some 2,500 years later the same ideal and stereotype can be found in similar and in additional aspects of modern-day culture and media, is history repeating itself, or are we in the midst of another trend? If current images of the male body are remnants of history, either as a repetition or a continuation, then certainly we face a tremendous challenge if we are to undo what has been done.

It is often impossible for us to repair the damage that has been caused by past civilizations or past deeds of humanity. With this in mind, the obvious course of our actions is *prevent* further damage.

This of course presumes that an idealized male body espoused as the ultimate man, lover, and mate in various areas of culture and media is causing or has caused some kind of damage, both physical and emotional, to men. This is an interesting debate because it pits those who, for the most part, control culture and media against themselves. It positions men against men in a world that usually or traditionally positions men against women.

Before the advent of a women's movement and the birth of feminism, a debate between men about how men should look to be socially accepted was missing from, or at least invisible in, society and culture. Because men were once in *total* control, no one cared how men looked physically, with or without their clothes. If anyone did care, male or female, few would dare to say so.

It can be argued that homosexual men of the past were the exceptions to this rule. They may have indeed cared about what other men looked like because they were interested in other men as partners and sexual playmates. However, these homosexual men, unlike a growing portion of today's homosexual culture, were compelled to remain silent for very different reasons, mainly their need to keep secret their true sexuality. Their maleness—the aspect of their being that kept them in control—was more important to them than their sexuality. For a homosexual man to openly discuss his emotional and sexual interest in other men was an immediate banishment from the ranks and privileges of being male. With such an admission, his maleness would be taken away; he would become, in the eyes of his still-in-control heterosexual male counterparts, as much a woman as a real woman. It was better to remain a real man by suppressing his true desires and adopting a facade closer in belief and meaning to the straight male majority; better to remain in control. What man, gay or straight, would want to be as inferior as a woman is so often treated?

It has always been difficult for men, past and present, to admit to being victims of anything, let alone victims of a beauty myth. The admission by men of victimization, in nearly any form, is likened to an act of demasculinization. For a man to admit that his self-worth and self-esteem are diminishing because he does not live up to current standards of male beauty removes the male self from the world of male domination and places the male self in the world of female submission. Idealized masculinity dictates that men cannot be victims of a beauty myth because to be such a victim means to feel some kind of emotional pain or suffering. Idealized masculinity allows and even encourages men's *physical* pain, but *emotional* pain, regardless of its source, is unmanly, feminine.

Power and control were once immune from the regimens of male beauty that have been created and implemented over the last decade or so. That immunity, however, has weakened and is beginning to crumble. Without the concurrent weakening and crumbling of male-dominated power and control in our society, this never would have happened. Since, however, men are slowly losing their hold on power and control, they are also beginning to lose a part of what gives them that power and control—their uncaring attitude toward how they appear physically, that is, their maleness. They are losing what women lost generations ago—the right to be the kind of women they choose to be, regardless of what society otherwise demands or dictates.

Women are not women—and have not been women for a long time—simply because they are born as females instead of males. Now men are not men simply because they are born as males instead of females. Our world has become far too complex and far too subjective to allow such simplistic definitions of men and women and of maleness and femaleness and of femininity and masculinity. Humanity is far too dependent upon collective sources of intellect and creativity to allow individual ideas and ideals of what qualifies men as men and women as women. In fact, individuality has all but disappeared from our society.

There is no doubt or question that women have suffered, and continue to suffer, from culturally imposed standards and stereotypes of female beauty. If this suffering were not real, there would not be seven million women currently tormented by serious, and often fatal, eating disorders. There would not be hundreds of thousands of cosmetic surgery procedures regularly performed on women in any given year. The diet industry would not be a multibillion-dollar industry. More than $20 billion would not be spent annually by women on cosmetics. Books such as Naomi Wolf's *The Beauty Myth* and Susan Faludi's *Backlash* would not have become national best-sellers and would not have sparked the debate and controversy they did.

We cannot undo what has been done to women. We can, however, prevent it from happening to present and future women. We can stop forcing women to pay these exorbitant and dangerous prices. We can learn from the mistakes we have made.

Because we know what culturally created, culturally imposed, and male-dominated ideals of physical beauty have done, and still can do, to women, men are, once again, afforded an opportunity not so easily given to women. Men can look at what has been and is being done to women and put a stop to it. Equally important, men can prevent the same from happening to them, if it is not too late. Surely men *can* do this. But *will* they?

To do this, men first will have to admit that a problem of idealized female physical appearance and beauty exists. Second, men will have to admit that the same problem exists or is beginning to exist in the male population. Women too will have to admit to the latter of these two aspects. Conceivably, it may be as difficult for women to admit to this as it is for men. Women also will have to admit that what is harmful to them is also harmful to men. It will do no good at all if women simply say that turnabout is fair play, or something similar.

If there is a war of the sexes raging in our society, and the object of that war is, on one side, to gain equality between the sexes and, on the other side, to maintain control, then surely this battle is ongoing, with no end in sight. Neither side can possibly win if either side is unwilling to change what is at stake. Men cannot maintain power if they allow women to have equal footing. Women cannot achieve equality if they allow men to maintain control. Where is the end? What is the hoped-for result or victory? Equality is not achieved when one side conquers and then seeks to reverse the power structure. Power is not maintained when one side succeeds in holding on to its power at the expense of keeping the other side where they have always been.

To reach an end or a conclusion, both men and women will need to change. However, to change the perception of the accepted male ideal into an equal perception of the accepted female ideal is not the change that is necessary. As Naomi Wolf says in *The Beauty Myth*, it is not women's bodies we need to change, it is the rules.[1]

What Wolf and others want is a change in the way we perceive women and in the way we perceive the female body. Wolf and the others want men to cease seeing women and the female body as the objects and results of their male-created fantasies, and they want women to stop accepting these fantasies as realities. No one is suggesting or demanding that women cease being beautiful or sexy. What is being suggested and demanded is the removal of the notion that women are worthy *only* if they live up to what others are telling them constitutes female beauty and female sexuality.

Women should not be considered beautiful and sexy because men tell them they are so but because they are rightfully deserving to be so or to believe themselves to be so. It must be *their own* ideas and versions defining beauty and sexiness, instead of and despite what others might think or say. Men must change how they see women, and women must change how they see themselves. Again, this is only one side of the problem and only one side of the solution.

The other side of this equation involves the male body and how the male body is viewed, both by women and men. What has become almost commonplace, even necessary, for women—cosmetic surgery, excessive dieting, eating disorders—has become equally customary for men. Will this hurt men as much as it has hurt women? It already has and will continue to do so unless, as Wolf suggests, the rules of our society change.

The burden of change, for men and for women, is placed upon those who feel compelled to alter their bodies or their appearance to fit within societal standards. Why not place the burden to change on society and how society perceives physical appearance? The fat or the ugly are expected to change how they look. Wouldn't it be better to change how society views and treats the fat and the ugly?

What women have lost—positive self-esteem, deserving self-worth—in a world and society fixated on physical beauty is a tragedy. To seek to prevent an equal tragedy for men is not to lessen in any way what has happened and continues to happen to women. Likewise, preventing the decline of men's self-esteem and self-worth can in no way make up or atone for what women have suffered. Yet if we can change the perception of the idealized or stereotyped male body that has permeated society, before it gets out of control, and in the process discover that similar treatment of the female body is wrong and harmful, perhaps we can finally find that elusive equal footing for which we have been searching.

If beauty is subjective—who can argue that it is not?—then we must let it be so. If we try to emulate or become what we see in the pockets of our culture, we are not allowing ourselves to be individually subjective. Instead, we are attempting to become someone other than who we are. In the process, we conclude that who we are is not suitable or worthy. We are quickly losing—perhaps have already lost—our innate right to self-define what is and is not beautiful or attractive to us, in us, and on us as individuals.

Unfortunately, we have allowed ourselves to become pieces of the cultural machinery that makes decisions for us. The art we view, the books we read, the advertisements we see, the films and television programs we watch—have become the teachers and we their students; we no longer inhabit a world in which people are capable of individual thought. Instead, we have become a place of collective subjectivity. In doing so, we have become lost, uncertain of who and what we are as single and important pieces of a collective humanity.

To make it all right depends, first, on whether we believe that something is wrong. This too is complicated by its own subjectivity. Right and wrong, and the definitions of each, are as debatable and controversial as beautiful and ugly. Few can deny the existing debate of what is and is not beautiful and ugly in women and whether the subject of that debate is in some way harmful to relationships between women and men and to women in general.

In addition, it cannot be denied that a similar debate has begun with respect to men, the beauty or ugliness of male bodies, and the potential harm to the relationships between men and women, men and men, and men in general. There appears to be little evidence to the contrary.

Where do we go from here? This question poses a tremendous challenge. It dares us to take a look at ourselves and to decide what we are doing, how we are living our lives, and what we have both assumed and given up as those things that do and might make us happy.

To look at ourselves, objectively and introspectively, can be a frightening experience. Self-examination means that we have to admit and deny what we and others say is right and wrong with us. What if the decisions we make about ourselves contradict what we and others have for so long believed? This is the chance we must take, the fear we must overcome and conquer. If we do not, nothing will change.

Perhaps it is arrogant and presumptuous to even suggest that a change is necessary in how the male body is projected and perceived in media and culture. After all, and when taken as a whole within our world, few are talking about the dangers—real or imagined—in creating ideals of male beauty. Even fewer are willing to admit that such a creation is or might become a problem.

If it is not a problem, then let us leave it alone. If it is, then let us find the courage to look inward and discover the beauty that waits for each of us.

Notes

Chapter 1

1. Naomi Wolf, *The Beauty Myth* (New York: Doubleday, 1991), p. 251.

2. Alan Farnham, "You're So Vain," *Fortune*, September 9, 1996, pp. 69, 74, 78, and 82.

3. Sam Keen and Ofer Zur, "Who Is the New Ideal Man?" *Psychology Today*, November 1989, p. 54.

4. Ibid.

5. Michael Pertschuk, Alice Trisdorfer, and Paul D. Allison, "How Men Measure Up," *Psychology Today*, November/December 1993, p. 54.

6. Louise Bernikow, "What Makes a Man Sexy Today?" *Cosmopolitan*, December 1987, p. 182.

7. Ibid., p. 183.

8. See Chris Sare, "What Makes a Man Sexy? Muscles, Mostly," *Muscle & Fitness*, January 1989, p. 165.

Chapter 2

1. Kenneth Clark, *The Nude: A Study in Ideal Form* (Princeton, NJ: Princeton University Press, 1990), pp. 30 and 32.

2. Margaret Walters, *The Nude Male* (New York: Paddington Press, 1978), p. 37.

3. Kenneth Clark, op. cit., p. 59.

4. Ibid., p. 103.

5. Ibid., p. 104.

6. Ibid., p. 257.

7. Susan Bordo, "Reading the Male Body," *The Michigan Quarterly Review*, Fall 1993, p. 726.

8. See Edward Lucie-Smith, *The Male Nude* (New York: Rizzoli, 1985). This is an excellent discussion on the male body in art.

9. Gill Saunders, *The Nude: A New Perspective* (New York: Harper & Row, 1989), p. 26.

10. Melody D. Davis, *The Male Nude in Contemporary Photography* (Philadelphia: Temple University Press, 1991), p. 13.

11. Tom Bianchi, *In Defense of Beauty* (New York: Crown Publishers, Inc., 1995), p. 8.

12. Ibid., p. 12.

13. Ibid., p. 18.
14. Ibid., p. 26.
15. Ibid., p. 31.
16. Ibid., p. 51.

Chapter 3

1. Edith Hamilton, *Mythology* (New York: Mentor, 1940), pp. 95-96.
2. Ibid., p. 96.
3. Ibid., pp. 101, 113, and 160.
4. Plato, *Symposium* (New York: Dover Publications, Inc., 1993), p. 21.
5. Nancy Friday, *The Power of Beauty* (New York: HarperCollins Publishers, Inc., 1996), p. 393.
6. Susannah Leigh, *Dawn Shadows* (New York: Penguin Books, Topaz Historical Romance, 1994), pp. 13-14, 17, and 23.
7. Ibid., p. 13.
8. Danielle Steel, *The Gift* (New York: Delacorte Press, 1994), pp. 47, 52, 55, 59, and 134.
9. Judith McNaught, *Until You* (New York: Pocket Books, 1994), p. 1.
10. Jane Smiley, *A Thousand Acres* (New York: Fawcett Columbine, 1991), pp. 9-10.
11. Ibid., pp. 103 and 156.
12. Robert James Waller, *The Bridges of Madison County* (New York: Warner Books, 1992), pp. 28 and 105.
13. Dennis E. Showalter, "Action! Adventure! Sales!" *Publishers Weekly*, May 3, 1989, p. 20.
14. Ibid.
15. Tom Clancy, *The Cardinal of the Kremlin* (New York: Berkley Books, 1989), p. 1.
16. John Grisham, *The Firm* (New York: Island Books, 1991), pp. 1-2, 31, 51, 153, and 158.
17. William Grimes, "Demigods Aren't Forever," *New York Times Magazine*, November 10, 1991, p. H1.
18. Anne Rice, *The Witching Hour* (New York: Ballantine Books, 1990), pp. 109, 139, 732, and 870.
19. Anne Rice, *Lasher* (New York: Ballantine Books, 1990), pp. 208 and 210.
20. Anne Rice, *The Witching Hour*, p. 1006.
21. Anne Rice, *The Mummy* (New York: Ballantine Books, 1989), pp. 69 and 71.
22. Ibid., p. 329.
23. E.M. Forster, *Maurice* (New York: W.W. Norton and Company, 1993), pp. 73 and 155.·
24. Oscar Moore, *A Matter of Life and Sex* (New York: Plume, 1991), pp. 9, 13, and 220.
25. Ibid., pp. 28 and 39.

26. Patricia Nell Warren, *The Front Runner* (New York: Penguin Books USA, Inc., 1988), pp. 26-27.

27. Ibid., pp. 4, 14, 31, and 79.

28. Ibid., p. 19.

29. Patricia Nell Warren, *Harlan's Race* (Los Angeles: Wildcat Press, 1994), pp. 11-12.

30. Ibid., pp. 27 and 41.

31. Ibid., pp. 52, 55, and 57-58.

32. Ibid., p. 75.

33. Ibid., p. 256.

34. Diane Goode, translation of Madame de Beaumont, *Beauty and the Beast* (New York: Bradbury Press, 1978), p. 23.

Chapter 4

1. Mark Simpson, "Hairy Fairies," *New Statesman & Society*, September 10, 1993, p. 34.

2. Quoted in Janice Castro, "Calvin Meets the Marlboro Man," *Time*, October 21, 1985, p. 69.

3. See Matthew Batstone, "Male Misgivings," *Marketing*, October 20, 1994, p. 20.

4. Betsy Sharkey, "Creating the New Man, Circa 1990: Advertising Defines and Refines the Male Image," *Adweek*, March 12, 1990, p. 36.

5. Mark Stuart Gill, "You've Come a Long Way, Buddy," *Working Woman*, March 1991, p. 77.

6. Ibid.

7. Betsy Sharkey, op. cit., p. 36.

8. The manufacturer of this particular cologne offers poster-size copies of the ad. Because this ad shows up in men's magazines, one has to wonder to what group of men the cologne, or at least the poster, is being marketed. It is difficult to imagine a straight man sending in six dollars so he can hang this poster in his home.

9. Robert Moritz, "Scent of a Man," *Gentlemen's Quarterly*, November 1994, p. 158.

10. See O.A.S.I.S. *Stale Roles and Tight Buns*, a video produced by a collective of men Organized Against Sexism and Institutionalized Stereotypes, O.A.S.I.S., 15 Willoughby Street, Boston, MA 02135, (617) 782-7769.

11. Joe Queenan, "Return of the Thin Man," *Men's Health*, January/February 1995, pp. 74 and 77.

12. Scott Omelianuk, "The Ultimate Dumbbell Workout," *Gentlemen's Quarterly*, October 1994, p. 176.

13. *Exercise for Men Only*, November 1994, p. 13.

14. Steve Downs, "Weight Training for Teens, Building a Strong Foundation," *Exercise for Men Only*, November 1994, p. 69.

15. Alan M. Klein, *Little Big Men: Bodybuilding Subculture and Gender Construction* (New York: State University of New York Press, 1993), p. 87.

16. Ibid., p. 87.

17. O.A.S.I.S., op. cit.

18. Naomi Wolf, *The Beauty Myth* (New York: Doubleday, 1991), p. 59. Italics are Wolf's.

19. Gerald Adams, quoted in Elaine Hatfield and Susan Sprecher, "Good Looks—What Is It?" In *Mirror, Mirror: The Importance of Looks in Everyday Life* (New York: State University of New York Press, 1986), p. 13.

20. Bernice Kanner, "Big Boys Don't Cry," *New York*, May 21, 1990, p. 20.

21. Paula Span, "Advertising's Lust Horizon," *The Washington Post*, February 26, 1994, p. D1.

22. Ibid., p. D6.

23. Janice Castro, op. cit., p. 69.

24. Paula Span, op. cit., p. D1.

25. Quoted in Benjamin Svetkey, "Here's the Beef," *Entertainment Weekly*, March 18, 1994, p. 26.

26. Quoted in Paula Span, op. cit., p. D6.

27. Naomi Wolf, op. cit., p. 289.

28. Vivian Gornick, Introduction to Erving Goffman's *Gender Advertisements* (New York: Harper & Row, 1987), p. 2.

29. O.A.S.I.S., op. cit.

Chapter 5

1. Marvin Jones, *Movie Buff Checklist: A History of Male Nudity in the Movies* (Los Angeles: Campfire Productions, 1993), p. 10.

2. Ibid., p. 24.

3. See Susan Jeffords, *Hard Bodies: Hollywood Masculinity in the Reagan Era* (New Brunswick, NJ: Rutgers University Press, 1994), p. 53.

4. See Susan Jeffords, ibid., for an excellent reference on masculinity as it is portrayed in Hollywood films. See also Steven Cohan and Ina Rae Hark (Eds.), *Screening the Male: Exploring Masculinities in Hollywood Cinema* (New York: Routledge, 1993).

5. See Marvin Jones, op. cit.

6. Susan Jeffords, op. cit., p. 34.

7. Ibid.

8. Antony Easthope, *What a Man's Gotta Do: The Masculine Myth in Popular Culture* (New York: Routledge, 1990), p. 53.

9. David Richards, "Jean-Claude Van Damme, the, uh, Actor?" *The New York Times*, September 4, 1994, p. H7.

10. Susan Jeffords, op. cit., p. 53.

11. Ibid., pp. 148-154.

12. See, for example, Philippa Pearce, *Beauty and the Beast* (New York: Thomas Y. Crowell Company, 1972); Marianne Mayer, *Beauty and the Beast* (New York: Four Winds Press, 1978); Diane Goode, *Beauty and the Beast* (New York: Bradbury Press, 1978); Rosemary Harris, *Beauty and the Beast* (New York:

Doubleday and Company, 1979); and Anne Carter, *Beauty and the Beast* (New York: Clarkson N. Potter, Inc., 1986).

13. See Susan Jeffords, op. cit.

14. Ibid.

15. Ibid., p. 152.

16. Ibid., p. 153.

17. Susan Jeffords, "Can Masculinity Be Terminated?" In Steven Cohan and Ina Rae Hark (Eds.), op. cit., p. 245.

18. Ibid.

19. Bruce Bibby, "Riddle Me This, Batman," *Premiere*, May 1995, p. 56.

20. See Robert James Waller, *The Bridges of Madison County* (New York: Warner Books, 1992), Chapter 2.

21. Rita Kempley, "'Madison County,' Iowa Corn," *The Washington Post*, June 2, 1995, p. D6.

22. Pat H. Broeske, "Wanted: New Action Stars," *The New York Times*, January 10, 1993, pp. H17 and H23.

Chapter 6

1. Peter J. Boyer, "TV Turns to the Hard-Boiled Male," *The New York Times*, February 16, 1989, Section 2, pp. 1 and 29.

2. Susan Faludi, *Backlash: The Undeclared War Against American Women* (New York: Anchor Books, 1991), p. 143.

3. Ibid., p. 145.

4. See Peter J. Boyer, op. cit., pp. 1 and 29. See also Susan Faludi, op. cit., p. 144.

5. Dennis McDougal, "TV's Guilty Pleasures," *TV Guide*, August 13, 1994, p. 12.

6. Ibid., p. 15.

7. Jeff Jarvis, "The Couch Critic," *TV Guide*, June 3, 1995, p. 9.

8. See Michael Logan, "Rapists: Unlikely Heartthrobs," *TV Guide*, June 19, 1994, p. 42.

9. Quoted on *Donahue*, Multimedia Entertainment, Inc., November 24, 1994.

10. Peter Watrous, "Pop Turns the Tables—with Beefcake," In *The New York Times*, February 10, 1991, p. 25.

11. Ibid. See also Barry Walters, "Music Videos Turn Up the Heat," *San Francisco Examiner*, January 24, 1993, p. D3.

12. See Fred Pfeil, "Rock Incorporated: Plugging into Axl and Bruce," *Michigan Quarterly Review*, Fall 1993, pp. 535-571.

13. See Barry Walters, op. cit. See also John Howell, "Jump Up the Volume, MTV's Best Boy Bodies," *Elle*, December 1992, p. 184.

Chapter 7

1. Scott MacDonald, "Confessions of a Feminist Porn Watcher," in Michael S. Kimmel (Ed.), *Men Confront Pornography* (New York: Meridian, 1991), p. 39.

2. Ibid., p. 37.

3. Whether or not women in pornography actually do desire men in pornography is irrelevant because a major focus of pornography is to create fantasy. The fact or nonfact that women who work in the pornography industry are somehow forced into the filmed sexual escapades is well beyond the scope of this discussion. Other books have covered this topic in great detail.

4. Scott MacDonald, op. cit., p. 38.

5. Harry Brod, "Eros Thanatized: Pornography and Male Sexuality," in Michael S. Kimmel (Ed.), op. cit., p. 198.

6. Ibid.

7. See Michael Pertschuk, Alice Trisdorfer, and Paul D. Allison, "How Men Measure Up," *Psychology Today,* November/December 1993, pp. 56 and 58. See also Jill Neimark, "The Beefcaking of America," *Psychology Today,* November/December 1994, pp. 70-71.

8. Men Against Pornography, "Is Pornography Jerking You Around?" In Michael S. Kimmel (Ed.), op. cit., p. 294.

9. Margaret Walters, *The Nude Male* (New York: Paddington Press, 1978), p. 291.

10. Letter to the Editor, *Playgirl,* December 1993, pp. 4-5.

11. Letter to the Editor, *Playgirl,* June 1994, pp. 6-7.

12. Letter to the Editor, *Playgirl,* November 1994, pp. 6-7.

13. Letter to the Editor, *Playgirl,* June 1994, p. 7.

Chapter 8

1. Lisa Rogak, "Why Does He Want to Starve?" *Weight Watchers Magazine,* June 1986, p. 61.

2. A. E. Andersen, Introduction, in Wolfgang Herzog, Hans-Christian Deter, Walter Vandereycken (Eds), *The Course of Eating Disorders, Long-Term Follow-up Studies of Anorexia and Bulimia Nervosa*, (New York: Springer-Verlag, 1992), p. 54.

3. Jean Seligmann, "The Pressure to Lose," *Newsweek*, May 2, 1994, p. 60.

4. Lisa Rogak, op. cit., p. 72.

5. A. E. Andersen, op. cit., p. 59. Other researchers also believe that gay men may be predisposed and/or particularly vulnerable to eating disorders, although no study has provided a definitive answer. See Joel Yager, Felice Kurtzman, John Landersverk, and Edward Wiesmeier, "Behaviors and Attitudes Related to Eating Disorders in Homosexual Male College Students," *American Journal of Psychiatry,* 145(4), April 1988, pp. 495-497; and Lisa Rogak, op. cit., p. 72.

6. Thomas E. Gettelman and J. Kevin Thompson, "Actual Differences and Stereotypical Perceptions in Body Image and Eating Disturbance: A Comparison of Male and Female Heterosexual and Homosexual Sample," *Sex Roles,* 29(7/8), 1993, p. 545.

7. Ibid., p. 546.

8. Judy Folkenberg, "Bulimia: Not for Women Only," *Psychology Today,* March 1984, p. 10.

9. Lisa Rogak, op. cit., pp. 72-73.

10. A. E. Andersen, op. cit., pp. 59, 61, and 63.

11. Gabriella Stern, "The Anorexic Man Has Good Reason to Feel Neglected," *The Wall Street Journal*, October 18, 1993, pp. A1 and A9.

12. Jean Seligmann, op. cit., pp. 60-61.

13. Jill Neimark, "The Beefcaking of America," *Psychology Today*, November/December 1994, p. 70.

14. Ibid.

15. A. E. Andersen, op. cit., p. 65.

Chapter 9

1. Figures provided by the American Society of Plastic and Reconstructive Surgeons, Arlington, IL.

2. Alan Farnham, "You're So Vain," *Fortune*, September 9, 1996, p. 68.

3. See Nora Underwood, "Sculpting the Body, Surgery Can Now Reduce Fat," *Macleans*, October 9, 1989, p. 58; Linda Troiano, "Skin, Scent & Hair," *American Health*, September 1990, p. 14; Rodney Ho, "Men Try to Put a New Face on Careers," *The Wall Street Journal*, August 28, 1991, pp. B1 and B4; Elizabeth Morgan, *The Complete Book of Cosmetic Surgery* (New York: Warner Books, 1988), p. 151; Ron Davis, "Forever Young," *Genre*, Fall 1991, p. 18; and Martha Sherrill, "Breast Him-Plants: The Joy of Pecs (the Lighter Side of a Heavy Issue)," *The Washington Post*, March 8, 1992, p. F1.

4. Cited in Naomi Wolf, *The Beauty Myth* (New York: Doubleday, 1991), p. 17.

5. See Rodney Ho, op. cit.

6. Patrick Folliard, "Standards of Beauty," *The Washington Blade*, August 21, 1992, p. 47.

7. Martha Sherrill, op. cit.

8. Patrick Folliard, op. cit.

9. Sheldon O. Burman, "The End of Impotence?" *Muscle & Fitness*, January 1993, p. 218.

10. Patrick Folliard, op. cit.

11. Elizabeth Morgan, op. cit., p. 320.

12. Ibid., p. 321.

13. Alan Farnham, op. cit.

14. Steve Schwade, "Body Shop," *Muscle & Fitness*, January 1993, p. 209.

15. Figure provided by the American Society of Plastic and Reconstructive Surgeons, Arlington Heights, IL.

16. Alan Farnham, op. cit.

17. Elizabeth Morgan, op. cit., p. 465.

18. Cited in Robin Marantz Henig, "Fat Suctioning: Surgeons Battle Over Who Should Do the Most Popular Cosmetic Operation in America," *Health: A Weekly Journal of Medicine, Science, and Society. The Washington Post*, April 4, 1989, p. 12.

19. Elizabeth Morgan, op. cit., p. 253.

20. Figure provided by the American Society of Plastic and Reconstructive Surgeons, Arlington, IL.

21. Elizabeth Morgan, op. cit. pp. 286-287.

22. Richard Laliberte, *Men's Health*, June 1991, p. 74.

23. Cited in Rodney Ho, op. cit.

24. Alan Farnham, op. cit.

25. Quoted in Emily Yoffe, "Valley of the Silicone Dolls," *Newsweek*, November 26, 1990, p. 72.

26. Martha Sherrill, op. cit.

27. Steve Schwade, op. cit.

28. Emily Yoffe, op. cit., p. 72

29. Emily Yoffe reports that a twenty-six-year-old Los Angeles fitness instructor opted for pectoral implants because "no amount of pumping iron could build up his puny pecs." See Emily Yoffe, op. cit., p. 72. See also Catherine Seipp, "A New You for the New Year," *The Advocate*, January 1, 1991, p. 49.

30. Quoted in Martha Sherrill, op. cit., p. F1.

31. Emily Yoffe, op. cit.

32. Simon Kinnerslay and C. E. Brietzke, "Made to Measure," *Men's Health*, April 1994, p. 64.

33. Ibid.

34. Ibid.

35. Ibid.

36. Naomi Wolf, op. cit., p. 257.

37. See Patrick Folliard, op. cit.

38. Naomi Wolf, op. cit., p. 232.

39. Elizabeth Morgan, op. cit., p. 4 (emphasis added).

Chapter 10

1. Cited in Alan M. Klein, *Little Big Men: Bodybuilding, Subculture and Gender Construction* (New York: State University of New York Press, 1993), p. 18.

2. Cited in Sam Fussell, "Bodybuilding Americanus," *Michigan Quarterly Review*, p. 577.

3. Alan M. Klein, op. cit., p. 18.

4. Jerry Kindela, "Turnin' the Tables," *Muscle & Fitness*, December 1992, p. 270.

5. Chris Sare, "Hard Bodies," *Muscle & Fitness*, September 1992, pp. 78 and 200.

6. See ibid., p. 204.

7. Armand Tanny, "Are Hard Bodies Sexier?" *Muscle & Fitness*, February 1991, pp. 94 and 189.

8. Jerry Kindela, op. cit., p. 138.

9. Armand Tanny, op. cit., p. 96.

10. Chris Sare, op. cit., p. 204.

11. "Molding Mr. Right," *People*, Summer 1991, p. 16.

12. Sam Fussell, op. cit., p. 586.

13. Armand Tanny, op. cit., p. 186.

14. Alan M. Klein, op. cit., p. 240.

15. Ibid. With the parenthetical remark that closes this quote, Klein is illustrating society's idea that weak and unmuscular men are considered effeminate. His book covers this subject extensively, quite effectively, and persuasively.

16. Ibid.

17. Ibid.

18. See Armand Tanny, op. cit., p. 188.

19. See ibid.

20. See ibid.

21. See Chris Sare, op. cit., p. 166.

22. See ibid., pp. 263-264.

23. Armand Tanny, op. cit., p. 188. See also Armand Tanny, "Why Women Love Muscular Men," *Muscle & Fitness*, August 1995, p. 180.

24. See Chris Sare, op. cit., p. 263.

25. See Armand Tanny, "Are Hard Bodies Sexier?" p. 189.

26. See Armand Tanny, "Why Women Love Muscular Men," p. 189.

27. See Armand Tanny, "Are Hard Bodies Sexier?" p. 180.

28. See Armand Tanny, "Why Women Love Muscular Men," p. 180.

29. Joe Weider, "Why Everyone Envies a Bodybuilder," *Muscle & Fitness*, June 1994, p. 180.

30. Ibid., p. 180.

31. See ibid.

32. See ibid.

33. See ibid.

34. See Sam Fussell, op. cit., p. 578.

35. See Joe Weider, op. cit., p. 180.

36. See Armand Tanny, "Are Hard Bodies Sexier?" p. 188, and Armand Tanny, "Why Women Love Muscular Men," p. 178.

37. Sam Fussell, op. cit., p. 593.

38. American College of Sports Medicine, "The Recommended Quantity and Quality of Exercise for Developing and Maintaining Cardiorespiratory and Muscular Fitness in Healthy Adults," 1990, p. 1.

39. Armand Tanny, "Are Hard Bodies Sexier?" p. 189 (emphasis added).

40. Sam Fussell, op. cit., pp. 578-579.

Chapter 11

1. Raymond M. Berger, *Gay and Gray* (Champaign, IL: The University of Illinois Press, 1982), p. 190.

2. Martin P. Levine (Ed.), *Gay Men: The Sociology of Male Homosexuality* (New York: Harper & Row, 1979), p. 7.

3. Quoted in Michael Nava, "Man 2 Man: The Battle of the Same Sexes," *Frontiers*, 11(15), November 20-December 4, 1992, p. 39.

4. Ibid., p. 40.

5. Ibid.

6. Brian Pronger, *The Arena of Masculinity: Sports, Homosexuality, and the Meaning of Sex* (New York: St. Martin's Press, 1990), p. 272.

7. Raymond M. Berger, op. cit., p. 14.

8. Seymour Kleinberg, *Alienated Affections* (New York: St. Martin's Press, 1980), p. 154.

9. Cited in Naomi Wolf, *The Beauty Myth* (New York: Doubleday, 1991), pp. 17 and 79.

10. A manager of a video store in San Francisco said that such information is not given out for "obvious reasons."

11. Naomi Wolf, op. cit., p. 132.

12. William J. Mann, "Laws of Desire: Has Our Imagery Become Over-Idealized?" *Metroline*, February 16-March 1, 1995, p. 22.

13. Richard D. Mohr, *Gay Ideas: Outing and Other Controversies* (Boston: Beacon Press, 1992), p. 148.

14. There are some in the gay male community who believe that body hair on men may be making a comeback. See Frank DeCaro, "The Fur Flies," *Genre*, April 1995, p. 12.

15. Frank Browning, *The Culture of Desire* (New York: Crown Publishers, Inc., 1993), p. 51.

16. Todd Simmons, "The Glamorization of AIDS," *The Advocate*, November 28, 1995, p. 29.

17. See Martin Merle, "David Kopay: Ten Years After," *Christopher Street,* 10(3), Issue 111, pp. 56-61.

18. See Michael Szymanski, "Battered Husbands: Domestic Violence in Gay Relationships," *Genre,* 1(3), Fall 1991, pp. 32, 44, and 73.

19. See Michael Nava, op. cit.

20. Frank Browning, op. cit., p. 193.

21. William J. Mann, op. cit.

22. William J. Mann, "Perfect Bound," *XY Magazine*, March 1996, p. 32.

Chapter 12

1. Naomi Wolf, *The Beauty Myth* (New York: Doubleday, 1991), p. 289.

Index

FORTHCOMING BOOKS
FROM HAWORTH GAY & LESBIAN STUDIES

TAKE 20% OFF EACH BOOK! *Special Sale!*

FROM TOADS TO QUEENS
Transvestism in a Latin American Setting
Jacobo Schifter, PhD
This crucial book adds important and new information against essentialist theories on the etiology of sexual orientation.
$39.95 hard. ISBN: 0-7890-0649-9.
$14.95 soft. ISBN: 1-56023-958-1.
Available Spring 1999. Approx. 161 pp. with Index.

MILITARY TRADE
Steven Zeeland
Challenges assumptions about both chaser and chased and poses pointed questions about the wisdom of those who seek to divide the world into "straight" and "gay."
$49.95 hard. ISBN: 0-7890-0402-X.
$19.95 soft. ISBN: 1-56023-924-7.
Available Spring 1999. Approx. 327 pp. with Index.

Over 300 Pages!

LOVE MATTERS
A Book of Lesbian Romance and Relationships
Linda Sutton, MA
From **Love Matters,** you'll receive honest, informative advice that can help you and your partner share a more open and fulfilling relationship.
$29.95 hard. ISBN: 0-7890-0288-4.
$14.95 soft. ISBN: 1-56023-918-2.
Available Spring 1999. Approx. 155 pp. with Index.

LONGTIME COMPANIONS
Autobiographies of Gay Male Fidelity
This book is a documentation of alternative lifestyles that richly fulfill personal needs as well as contribute to the community.
$39.95 hard. ISBN: 0-7890-0641-3.
$24.95 soft. ISBN: 1-56023-957-3.
Available Spring 1999. Approx. 220 pp. with Index.

Over 200 Pages!

IN YOUR FACE
Stories from the Lives of Queer Youth
You'll see how these young persons experience and define their lives, their views, and their visions of their futures.
$29.95 hard. ISBN: 0-7890-0076-8.
$17.95 soft. ISBN: 1-56023-887-9.
Available Spring 1999. Approx. 184 pp. with Index.

TRAILBLAZERS
Profiles of America's Gay and Lesbian Elected Officials
Kenneth E. Yeager, PhD
A quick reference to the most comprehensive list of the country's 124 openly gay and lesbian officials. You'll read about 11 of these representatives in greater depth, getting to know them personally and professionally.
$29.95 hard. ISBN: 0-7890-0299-X.
Text price (5+ copies): $24.95.
Available Winter 1998/99. Approx. 220 pp. with Index.
Features interviews, a chronology of the advancement of elected gay officials, addresses of 'out' gay and lesbian officials, and appendixes.

Over 200 Pages!

IT'S A QUEER WORLD
Deviant Adventures in Pop Culture
Mark Simpson
"This book is one of the most entertaining ever written on popular culture and sexuality."
—*Gay Times*
$39.95 hard. ISBN: 0-7890-0609-X.
$14.95 soft. ISBN: 1-56023-950-6.
Available Winter 1998/99. Approx. 194 pp.
Includes recommended reading.

NAVIGATING DIFFERENCES
Friendships Between Gay and Straight Men
Jammie Price, PhD
Explores the gender and sexual identities of gay and straight men who become friends and how those identities influence their behavior with one another.
$24.95 hard. ISBN: 0-7890-0619-7.
Text price (5+ copies): $17.95.
Available Winter 1998/99. Approx. 179 pp. with Index.
Features numerous interviews, surveys, interview checklists, and 4 appendixes.

IN THE PINK
The Making of Successful Gay- and Lesbian-Owned Businesses
Sue Levin, MBA
Offers a real-life view of gay and lesbian business ownership, with insights from over 650 gay and lesbian entrepreneurs into why and how they started their businesses and how they currently manage them.
$24.95 hard. ISBN: 0-7890-0579-4.
$17.95 soft. ISBN: 1-56023-941-7.
Available Winter 1998/99. Approx. 180 pp. with Index.
Features case studies, numerous interviews, tables, a list of organizations, Web site/Internet addresses, and survey methodology and recommended books.

BEHOLD THE MAN
The Hype and Selling of Male Beauty in Media and Culture
Edisol Wayne Dotson
The first comprehensive study of how images of male beauty are projected onto society, and the role media and society play in creating the image of the idealized male.
$29.95 hard. ISBN: 0-7890-0634-0.
$19.95 soft. ISBN: 1-56023-953-0.
Available Winter 1998/99. Approx. 173 pp. with Index.
Features recommended readings; reviews of articles, books, and films; and television and print advertising critiques, evaluations, and interpretations.

WE'RE ONLINE!
Visit our online catalog and search for publications of interest to you by title, author, keyword, or subject! You'll find descriptions, reviews, and complete tables of contents of books and journals
http://www.haworthpressinc.com

 **Harrington Park Press,**
An Imprint of The Haworth Press, Inc.
10 Alice Street, Binghamton, New York 13904–1580 USA